WELFARE REFORM

Other Books in the At Issue Series:

WELFARE REFORM

David Bender, *Publisher*
Bruno Leone, *Executive Editor*

Scott Barbour, *Managing Editor*
Brenda Stalcup, *Series Editor*

Charles P. Cozic, *Book Editor*

An Opposing Viewpoints ® Series

Greenhaven Press, Inc.
San Diego, California

Library of Congress Cataloging-in-Publication Data

Welfare reform / Charles P. Cozic, book editor.
        p.   cm. — (At issue)
    Includes bibliographical references and index.
    ISBN 1-56510-546-X (lib. : alk. paper). — ISBN 1-56510-545-1
(pbk. : alk. paper)
    1. Public welfare administration—United States. 2. Public
welfare—United States. 3. United States—Social policy. I. Cozic,
Charles P., 1957–   . II. Series: At issue (San Diego, Calif.)
HV95.W4545   1997
361.973—dc20   96-33567
                                                                      CIP

© 1997 by Greenhaven Press, Inc., PO Box 289009,
San Diego, CA 92198-9009

Printed in the U.S.A.

Table of Contents

Introduction

In August 1996, Bill Clinton fulfilled his 1992 campaign pledge to "end welfare as we know it" when he signed the Personal Responsibility and Work Opportunity Reconciliation Act. Upon signing this landmark law (after twice vetoing similar legislation submitted by the Republican-controlled Congress), Clinton announced, "We are taking an historic chance to make welfare what it was meant to be: a second chance, not a way of life."

Most Americans—including members of Congress—welcomed legislation ending the federal government's unlimited entitlement program known as Aid to Families with Dependent Children (AFDC). The backbone of the 1996 act—time limits as short as thirty days on cash assistance to the nonworking poor—was a feature that had appeared in both Clinton's proposed Work and Personal Responsibility Act of 1994, which Congress declined to vote on, and the Republicans' Personal Responsibility Act of 1995, which Clinton vetoed in January 1996.

Efforts to reform America's welfare system had been gaining momentum since the late 1980s, when President Ronald Reagan and others asserted that AFDC and other federal welfare programs had grossly failed to help the poor. These critics argued that states should receive federal waivers to create their own programs to encourage welfare recipients to find work.

In 1988, Wisconsin became the first state to pursue substantial welfare reform when it received a federal waiver of AFDC rules for its "Learnfare" program, which reduced AFDC benefits to welfare families whose teenage children were excessively truant from school. In 1994, it became the first state to deauthorize AFDC in favor of a state-designed alternative called Wisconsin Works. The new plan, taking effect in 1997, bases aid on recipients' efforts to secure employment rather than providing recipients with unconditional entitlements. Republicans, as well as Clinton, praised Wisconsin's pilot program.

Wisconsin's precedent-setting plan provided a model for state and congressional architects of welfare reform. The thrust of the 1996 welfare act transfers control over welfare spending—after decades of federal oversight—to the states, granting them permission to initiate programs similar to Wisconsin's. In addition to providing federal welfare "block grants" to states to spend at their discretion, the act permits states to halt payments to teen mothers who do not live either at home or in a supervised setting or who drop out of school. States can also deny increased benefits to mothers who have additional children while on welfare. Although many advocates argue that state control will prove more effective than the federal government in helping the poor get off welfare, critics contend that states will drastically cut welfare benefits and that some federal control is necessary to ensure adequate assistance for the needy.

According to proponents of increased state control, state governments are better suited to assist their poor citizens than is the federal government. They contend that, through what the 1996 welfare act terms "broad cash welfare and child care block grants" totaling no more than $16.4 billion annually, states can custom-design programs to meet the needs of the poor, including helping them find work. American Enterprise Institute scholar Douglas J. Besharov maintains that leaving welfare reform to the states "is an exceedingly good idea. The federal government doesn't really bring very much to the program except money." Heritage Foundation welfare expert Robert Rector writes:

> By combining dozens of federal welfare programs into block grants to the states, eliminating tens of thousands of pages of federal regulations, and letting governors and state legislators take direct responsibility and do what they think is best for their communities, welfare reform can serve low-income people more efficiently.

Many commentators agree that the states will serve the poor more effectively. Indeed, welfare-reform advocates credit stricter state welfare initiatives for contributing to the 9 percent decrease (1.3 million individuals) in America's welfare caseload from 1993 to 1996. In the words of Massachusetts governor William Weld, the federal government is correct to "get out of the way" and let the states conduct their own welfare programs. Weld notes that in 1995, the first year of his state's welfare-reform program, the AFDC caseload decreased by almost 16 percent.

However, opponents of increased state control believe that the federal government is better situated to meet the needs of the poor. Congressmember Major R. Owens, a New York Democrat, argues that states do not have the power of the federal Treasury, "which guarantees that no matter how bad the economic conditions may be and how many people may be forced on welfare, the money will be made available to meet their needs." Moreover, Columbia University political science professor Demetrios Caraley observes that "federal funding of safety net programs means that the cost of helping the disadvantaged can be shared by taxpayers throughout the country, as are the costs of natural disasters."

Critics of state control insist that state programs will harm poor people. According to Owens, "Block grants place the poor at the mercy of state and local governments. [Federally funded] school lunches were created in the first place because state and local governments refused to meet [children's] needs." Many fear that states' lack of accountability over welfare spending threatens to push the poor deeper into poverty. They maintain that, pressed to make budget cuts and having been given the freedom to cut benefits sharply, states could slash cash payments and services to the poor. Such action would weaken, if not destroy, the financial safety net that the poor have been guaranteed for decades, these critics contend. In the words of welfare-rights activist Betty Reid Mandell, "We know what the states do with welfare when they decide to cut back expenses—they cut it."

Concerned that state initiatives could adversely affect some of the poor, Clinton has proposed to "change what is wrong" in the 1996 welfare act while retaining the basic reforms. Although the selections included in this anthology were written prior to the passage of the Personal Responsibility and Work Opportunity Reconciliation Act, they present cogent arguments for and against measures that are contained in the act and other proposed reforms of the welfare system. The authors in *At Issue: Welfare Reform* debate the potential positive and negative effects of creating stricter welfare programs for America's poor.

1

Poor Women and Children Need Welfare

Betty Reid Mandell

Betty Reid Mandell has been a welfare-rights activist since the 1960s. She coedits the newspaper Survival News, *written by and about poor people, and is the author of several books on social welfare issues.*

Many poor Americans and other concerned individuals fear that welfare-reform proposals and cuts in welfare benefits will make the lives of poor women and children more miserable. Because of the scarcity of jobs that pay a livable wage, impoverished Americans need programs such as Aid to Families with Dependent Children (AFDC), job training, and food stamps. The poor should not be criticized or scapegoated for depending on these welfare programs to survive. To help poor mothers, government should improve AFDC, expand the economy, and strive to provide universal health insurance and day care.

David Stockman, Ronald Reagan's budget director, predicted the future when he said, "There are *no* entitlements, *period!*" The goal of the Republicans then, as now, was to destroy the idea that the government owed *anything to the people.* Once that is accomplished, the safety net of the U.S. welfare state, never very strong compared to those in Europe, can be shredded entirely. Then, there is no buffer to protect people from having to take any low-waged job, or to protect women from having to remain in a painful marriage, or even to protect them from homelessness.

The dismantling of the welfare state is not just a Republican venture. Although they have been the most aggressive about it, the Democrats have done their share. But the Newt Gingrich [House of Representatives speaker] Republicans have dealt a body blow to Aid to Families with Dependent Children (AFDC), the main program of support for poor children and their parents, by their passage of the Personal Responsibility Act. This Act would convert the AFDC program into a federal block grant and turn the program over to the states with fixed funding for each of the next five years. If the Senate passes that Act and the President signs it [Bill Clinton vetoed it in January 1996], entitlements are over and state discretion is

Betty Reid Mandell, "Shredding the Safety Net," *New Politics*, Summer 1995. Reprinted with permission.

the order of the day. The federal/state cooperation in the program that has been in place since the original Social Security Act of 1935 is ended. No child would be assured of receiving help in times of need—regardless of the depth of the child's poverty or the parents' willingness to work.

The Republicans call it devolution. George Will, writing in *Newsweek*, boasted that it would send power "back to where it came from and belongs, back to the people and their state governments." They say it will give states more flexibility to suit the program to local conditions. They even claim that it will help move people out of poverty and change their behavior. Yet there is not a shred of evidence that a block grant will either move people out of poverty or change their behavior and attitudes. What the block grant says is that people who play by the rules, whatever they may be, will be denied benefits arbitrarily when state politicians cannot decide on a tax increase or a local aid cut or whatever when a fiscal crisis occurs.

We know what the states do with welfare when they decide to cut back expenses—they cut it. The program that is funded entirely by states, General Assistance (GA), is always the first welfare program to be cut, even before AFDC (a state/federal matching program) is cut. The General Assistance program (sometimes called General Relief) is for people who do not qualify for AFDC or other entitlement programs—disabled people in the process of applying for Supplemental Security Income (SSI) or Social Security Disability Insurance (SSDI); unemployed, able-bodied individuals with little or no income who are ineligible for unemployment insurance benefits; and poor two-parent families whose primary wage-earner lacks a recent work history. Not all states even have the program. The Center on Budget and Policy Priority points to a 1992 survey which showed nine states with no GA program and ten other states that had GA programs only in some parts of the state. Even the 31 states and the District of Columbia did not cover all—or even close to all—categories of needy people and the level of aid was very low, a median of $215 a month, 36% of the poverty line.

During the 1991–1992 recession, Michigan abolished its General Relief program, ending benefits for about 82,000 recipients, and Illinois cut off benefits for about 66,000 GA recipients. Rhode Island abolished its program. Ohio ended aid after six months. Several other states cut back the program in various ways. Follow-up studies in Michigan and Ohio showed that relatively few former GA recipients became employed after their benefits were ended and those who did were in low-wage and often temporary jobs. In Michigan, there was a 50 percent increase in homelessness. In Ohio, the ranks of the homeless increased substantially.

The Personal Responsibility Act

The Personal Responsibility Act (PRA) of the Contract With America [a collection of proposed conservative Republican reforms] would attach some tight strings to the AFDC program before turning it back to the states. Couching their language in phrases that seem benignly protective of poor people's character, they promise to "end dependency" by getting women off the rolls by forcing them to work. They claim that their bill will increase women's self-sufficiency. They further promise to "strengthen family values" and end illegitimacy by denying support to unmarried teen mothers. At first, they threatened to put some children into orphanages if mothers could not care for them, but in the final version of the PRA, there was no mention of orphanages. And they promise to discourage women from having babies while they are on the dole by denying support to babies born to a mother who receives AFDC. They claim that all of this will reduce poverty.

Taking away the economic life-line of poor women and children will only make their lives vastly more miserable than they already are.

This is voodoo social science. Taking away the economic life-line of poor women and children will only make their lives vastly more miserable than they already are on AFDC grants that are 50% below the poverty line. Women and children will swell the ranks of the homeless. But the Personal Responsibility Act brandishes a sword over women's heads, telling them that they had better get a man or a job to support them, *or else*. Following is a summary of its main provisions, as explained by the Center on Budget and Policy Priorities:

• Lumps monies from AFDC and Emergency Aid to Families into block grants paid to states with virtually no federal government oversight and with no requirement that states provide matching funds.

• Sets a "drop dead" five-year lifetime limitation on cash assistance and workfare slots. Most families would be *permanently* banned from receiving any further assistance from the block grant. All parents who have received cash aid for two years will be required to participate in "work activities," as defined by the state. A specified percentage of the adult caseload must participate in a work program—50 percent by 2003. At least one parent in 90 percent of two-parent families would be required to participate. Parents may also participate in training, but must also do one other work activity for at least 20 hours a week (30 hours for adults in two-parent families).

States would be required to end both cash assistance and workfare slots for families who had received AFDC for five years. States could end assistance after two years. After their limit has been reached, families could not receive assistance again *for a lifetime*. The PRA would not provide jobs, education, or job training. It provides for no exemptions from work. States could require parents caring for disabled children or infants to work full time.

A large fraction of recipients would be required to work their AFDC benefits off for 35 hours a week at "wages" that would equal $2.42 an hour for a family of three in the typical state. Nationally nearly half of all children receiving assistance today—or about 4.5 million children—are in families that have received benefits for a cumulative total of five years. The five-year cut-off would make millions of poor children ineligible for federal aid.

The Center on Budget and Policy Priorities says, "The bill includes a perverse incentive that allows states to meet their work participation rates simply by denying large numbers of families cash assistance under the block grant. If a state simply denied assistance to one-half of its caseload, it would reduce by one-half the number of parents that would be required to participate in the work program."

• Prohibits states from using federal block grant funds to provide cash assistance to children born to a family already receiving aid or to a family that received aid at any time during the 10-month period before the birth of the child. *The child would remain ineligible for aid throughout his or her childhood.* The Department of Health and Human Services estimates that this provision would ultimately deny aid to more than 2 million children a year.

• Eliminates cash assistance provided through the Supplemental Security Income (SSI) program for the 80 percent of the low-income disabled children who would otherwise become eligible for aid in future years, including children suffering from disabilities such as Down Syndrome and cerebral palsy. The Congressional Budget Office estimates that about 80 percent of low-income disabled children who would have become eligible for SSI assistance in the future would be denied aid under this bill. Under current law, about 1.25 million children are projected to receive SSI benefits by the year 2000. Under this bill, only about 500,000 children would receive SSI.

[Bill Clinton's] Work and Family Responsibility Act emphasized low-wage or forced work rather than education and training.

• Denies AFDC and housing benefits to unmarried mothers who have a child before their 18th birthday, and would allow states to deny cash aid and/or housing assistance to unmarried mothers under 21. This will deny aid to 70,000 children a year, according to a Department of Health and Human Services estimate.

• Rewards states by granting them up to a 10% increase if they reduce their "illegitimacy ratio," the ratio of live births to out-of-wedlock births and the sum of abortions in the general population.

• Reduces the cash grants of families that include a child for whom legal paternity has not been established by the state. Even when the mother has fully cooperated with the child support agency but the state has been unable to establish paternity, the family's grant would be reduced by $50 or 15 percent, whichever is less.

• Merges federal food assistance programs including the school lunch and Women, Infants, and Children (WIC) programs into a block grant and sets the block grant's funding level several billion dollars below what is needed to maintain current benefits. The school lunch and school breakfast programs would no longer be entitlement programs.

• Cuts $23 billion from the Food Stamp program over five years. Sets a 90-day time limit for people 18–50 years old to receive Food Stamps. Includes a work requirement. While agribusiness and food corporations succeeded in keeping Food Stamps out of a block grant, Congress compromised with their lobbyists and allowed states to take over the Food Stamp program if they set up an electronic transfer system.

• Makes poor *legal* immigrants ineligible for about 60 federally-funded health, education, job training, housing, social service, and income security programs. About the only program they could still get is emergency medical services.

• Replaces federal child welfare programs, including foster care and adoption assistance, with a block grant. The Congressional Budget Office estimates that the federal financial commitment to abused and neglected children will be reduced by $1.7 billion from 1995 to 2000.

• Repeals the current Job Opportunities and Basic Skills (JOBS) program which requires states to provide a range of education, training, and work programs for AFDC parents.

• Reduces federal resources for child care. At the same time that states are supposed to place more parents in work programs, the child care assistance will be reduced.

• Denies SSI benefits to *all* persons disabled by drug or alcohol abuse. In 1994, Congress (both Republicans and Democrats) enacted tough legislation to limit disability benefits for substance abusers under the SSI and Social Security disability programs. SSI recipients can only get assistance for three years, and are required to participate in treatment programs as a condition of receiving benefits.

• Imposes spending caps on many important programs for the poor, including AFDC, Supplemental Security Income (SSI), child support enforcement, child care programs, and child protection programs. The caps are well below what is spent now, and spending would continue to be cut in future years.

The Department of Health and Human Services estimates that ultimately about half of the children, perhaps as many as 6 million, who receive AFDC under current law would be denied benefits due to the time limit, the child exclusion provision, or the provision denying aid to minor mothers and their children. Net reductions in programs under the PRA would amount to $65 billion over five years. These reductions in funding, they add, "represent a significant retreat in the federal government's commitment to protect vulnerable children and provide a safety net for poor families."

Clinton's proposals

President Clinton made a weak protest about the Contract With America hurting children, but engaged in some macho posturing himself by saying the Republicans were not tough enough on work. His Work and Responsibility Act of 1994 called for a two-year time limit on AFDC, but recipients who had received two years of cash assistance would be required to work. If they could not find an unsubsidized job, they would be provided a subsidized work slot (workfare) and paid at least the federal minimum wage. Clinton's plan also called for parents who are minors to live at home or in a specified setting in order to get assistance; allowed states to implement a "Learnfare" program, cutting benefits if children fail to meet school attendance requirements; denied aid to children born while a mother is on AFDC; and denied aid to a mother who cannot name the father of her child.

When he was campaigning for president, Clinton talked of the importance of providing education and training to help welfare recipients succeed in the workplace and leave welfare for good. As Governor of Arkansas and chairman of the National Governors Association, Clinton helped shape the Family Support Act of 1988 which includes education and training. Now, however, Clinton has moved away from this position. His Work and Family Responsibility Act emphasized low-wage or forced work rather than education and training.

Twenty years ago, Ralph Nader warned that the Republicans were engaged in a campaign to undermine people's trust in government so they could dismantle it, since it sometimes prevented the worst depredations of capitalism. Now we see how prescient Nader was. The Republicans, often aided by the Democrats, have succeeded in creating widespread mistrust of government. They have also succeeded in creating, or at least exacerbating, widespread mistrust of the poor. The two together create an explosive mixture that has led to a terroristic campaign against all poor people, but especially AFDC mothers, and particularly teenage mothers. Having created their designated scapegoats to draw the public's hostility, politicians, in the service of corporate interests, were free to close in for the kill and take away the supports that made it possible for the poor, at least, to survive. Corporate welfare went almost unnoticed while the public cried for the blood of welfare mothers.

The divide-and-conquer diversionary tactic worked. A flood of conservative rhetoric condemned the "dependency" of people who got help from the government and who "didn't work." They never conceded that caring for children is work, unless it is caring for other people's children for pay. Welfare mothers were pictured as lazy and immoral, breeding children simply to get more welfare money. People who were stressed-out by falling wages, disappearing jobs, overwork, and lack of health insurance and child care, turned on those "lazy dependents" who seemed to be abetted by government "handouts." They let the Savings and Loan (S & L) crooks off the hook, even though the money lost could have paid for AFDC in all 50 states for nearly seven years. The federal and state spending on AFDC is about $22 billion a year, $128 billion less than the government spent on the bailout resulting from the Savings and Loan scandal. But the media feature endless stories about the dependency and fraud of welfare moms, not the dependency and fraud of S & L thieves. Nor does the media pay much attention to the vendors—agencies and professionals such as doctors, dentists, and pharmacists who serve welfare clients and who commit 93% of the welfare fraud in Massachusetts.

The war against women

The economic warfare against the poor is combined with cultural warfare. Charles Murray, a man who seems crazed by the thought of teenagers having sex, has provided the theoretical underpinnings of much of the Personal Responsibility Act (if one can call his pseudo-science, palmed off as "research," theory). He blames teenage mothers for most of society's ills and claims to believe that depriving them of AFDC grants will prevent their getting pregnant. Of course that is absurd. But it will help to restigmatize having babies without getting married, which is what the right wing quite clearly says that it wants to do. Title I of the Personal Responsibility Act is entitled, "Reducing Illegitimacy." It declares that "marriage is the foundation of a successful society," and goes on to give a laundry list of "facts" about illegitimacy which features teenage mothers and links criminality with absent black fathers. States have joined in this warfare against teen parents, passing laws restricting welfare and giving them rewards (dubbed "Bridefare" or "Wedfare" programs) if they marry any man, not necessarily the father of their child.

AFDC does not encourage family breakup and out-of-wedlock births.

Welfare is one of the battlegrounds of the war on women. The National Organization for Women (NOW) has organized a "Committee of One Hundred" to fight against punitive welfare legislation. They say that not only does the Personal Responsibility Act wreak its havoc on poor women and their children, but it also "suggests a broader effort to pressure all women into a repressive sexuality, limited reproductive choices, and conventional family arrangements." The radical right understands the connection between a safety net and women's autonomy. By withdrawing federal assistance for women without male support (and by also attacking affirmative action, Title IX [which outlaws discrimination based on sex], and college financing), by branding welfare mothers with demeaning racial stereotypes, by pauperizing them and questioning their fitness as mothers, the right is pressuring all women to depend economically on men within a traditional marriage whether or not they want to, and whether or not the men are dependable. The economic alternative is so harsh that women may find themselves unable to provide for their families and have to give up their children to foster care or adoption.

AFDC does not encourage family breakup and out-of-wedlock births. Single-parent households are on the rise but it is not due to AFDC. While the value of the AFDC benefit fell during the last 20 years, the number of mother-only households rose.

Unwed teenage mothers comprise a small portion of welfare mothers. Only 11 percent of welfare mothers are teenagers, of whom 65 percent live with their own parents, and 20 percent live with other adults. Unwed motherhood is on the rise due to divorce, delayed marriage, changing sexual norms, the falling standard of living, and other social conditions. The problem of teenage pregnancy has been vastly overstated and misrepresented. The teenage birthrate declined 20 percent between 1970 and 1984. Even as late as 1990, the teenage birthrate was just about back where it had been at the beginning of the 1970s.

If abortion were easily available to poor women, there would be fewer out-of-wedlock births. Predictably, the Hyde Amendment [introduced by Illinois representative Henry Hyde] resulted in more births to low-income mothers by prohibiting federal funding for abortions. Sharon Thompson, writing in the *New York Review of Books*, noted that in the late 1970s, before the right to life movement interfered, pregnancy and maternity rates fell to their lowest level since the 1940s. They began to rise as abortion became increasingly stigmatized and restricted, and the harder it has become to obtain abortion in a given state, the higher the teenage pregnancy rate. While the Reagan and Bush administrations' anti-abortion stance stigmatized *pregnancy*, the Clinton Administration, along with the Republican Congress, stigmatizes *motherhood*.

Teenagers are more likely to have babies when they see no other future for themselves. Those who go on to higher education or fulfilling careers are not as likely to have babies as those who drop out of high school. President Clinton acknowledges that the best approach to birth control in Third World countries is to educate the women, but he does not apply that insight to teenagers in the U.S. In European countries there is, by and large, as much teenage sex as there is in the U.S., but many fewer babies are born as a result of it. That is because Europeans give early and adequate sex education and contraception in schools, and have a healthier and less ambivalent attitude toward sex.

All these policies limit the choices of poor women, and further deepen the rift between poor women who have no choices and affluent women who do. These reproductive issues affect only poor women now, but they are related to the drive to limit reproductive choice for *all* women. Katha Pollitt of the *Nation* points out that the conservative talk about putting poor children into orphanages is not really about orphanages, but about women—about reinforcing the sexual double standard.

Universal vs. means-tested programs

There are about 3 million children who receive Social Security benefits, along with their parents. These children are the dependents of retired, deceased, or disabled workers or are themselves disabled. Most people are not even aware of the existence of these "dependents." Certainly their mothers are not subjected to scrutiny of their sex lives, work habits, housekeeping standards, or budgeting and shopping skills. That is because Social Security is a "universal" benefit, that is, everyone whether rich or poor is entitled to the benefit if they meet the basic qualifications, and over 90% of the population does. Universal programs have much stronger political support than do means-tested programs which are only for the poor. People who receive Social Security are called "claimants"; people who receive AFDC are called "recipients." As the late great British social welfare scholar, Richard Titmuss, said, "Programs for the poor are poor programs." Universal programs, however, are not invulnerable (nothing is), and we see both the Republicans and the Democrats itching to slash Social Security and Medicare. Congress has already cut vulnerable and little noticed populations from Social Security, such as college students and many of the disabled. They also reduced benefits for the very poor by eliminating the minimum level for benefits of $122 a month.

In her book, *Pitied but Not Entitled*, Linda Gordon argues that the deserving/undeserving, universal/means-tested split was built into the Social Security law at its inception because of the differing philosophies of the men who developed the universal parts of the Act and the women who developed the means-tested ADC [Aid to Dependent Children]. The women were social workers who directed the Children's Bureau. Although they had been heavily influenced by the suffrage movement and helped to create many programs for children, they shared the elitism and racism of many in the Progressive movement. They felt morally superior to immigrants and blacks, and as social workers they felt it their duty to supervise them on an individual, case-by-case basis. They envisioned a small program with "nice" women, mostly widows and their children. They thought of it as a temporary program, presumably until women remarried. They ignored the large numbers of single mothers who could not or would not rely on a man for support.

The media are willing accomplices of business interests and public officials in stereotyping "welfare moms."

The men who created the Social Insurance program, on the other hand, wanted a program to which workers were *entitled*. They were not interested in people's character flaws. Many of them were from Europe and had studied Germany's social insurance system. They developed the unemployment compensation system, workers' compensation, and Old Age Insurance. But they shaped a program that responded to the needs of working men, and the elite of the working class—those with steady jobs with major employers, and professionals. It left out single mothers, the working poor who had low wages, and the workers who were not wage earners like farmers, sharecroppers, and small businessmen. Only much later were those people included. Women homemakers were never included in their own right, only as dependents of their husbands.

The framers of social insurance did not like the fact that ADC was means-tested rather than an entitlement program, and that it required supervision of clients. They were correct in believing that only by making social insurance a universal program could it avoid the "stigma of the dole and the humiliation of dependence." Yet, while creating a non-stigmatized program for the workers' male elite, they never seriously considered a universal program that would include housewives, sharecroppers, or domestic servants. To build political support for their program, they even created hostility in the public mind about the means-tested ADC program, thereby increasing its stigma. ADC (later called AFDC) continued as a stigmatized means-tested program giving its *recipients* much less money than social insurance *claimants* received, and scapegoating them as the "unworthy poor."

Women reformers criticized social insurance because it was based on insuring wage earners (leaving out women who cared for children), and was based on the assumption that women would be taken care of by men's insurance. Yet both the men and the women agreed with the concept of the "family wage," i.e., that a male worker's wage should be enough to support him and his family, while his wife should stay home to care for the children. The "family wage" ignored the many single mothers who had to support their family alone without the help of a man. The women were "maternalists," who framed their fight for poor women in terms of the needs of children rather than in terms of the mothers' right to an independent income. This weakened their position, since officials argued that the state was not *obliged* to meet those needs. It also meant that *mothers'* needs were ignored. The ADC program began in 1935 but did not include mothers until 1950. This strategy of appealing to people's pity for children and ignoring the mothers is similar to the strategy of the Children's Defense League (CDL) today. In an effort to placate conservative lawmakers and gain public sympathy, the League has emphasized the needs of children rather than the rights of mothers to compensation for their service as caretakers. It promoted children's nutrition programs and Head Start, but did not defend AFDC. As a result, the CDL left AFDC mothers, along with their children, undefended and at the mercy of right-wing assault without any support.

The men who framed the social insurance part of the Social Security Act were responding to powerful social movements from the grassroots, including workers' militancy, the Townsend movement, Huey Long's movement, and the unemployed movement. The women who framed the ADC program had no women's movement to support them in the 1930s. Poor single mothers had no movement to advance their claims in the political arena until the welfare rights movement of the 1960s and 1970s. The second wave of the women's movement virtually ignored them until about 1993, when the National Organization for Women (NOW) took up their cause. Only after they recognized the threat in the Contract With America did single-issue reproductive rights groups, such as the National Abortion Rights Action League (NARAL), begin to fight for the reproductive rights of mothers on welfare. They had not at first fought vigorously against the Hyde amendment, but they now recognize it as an assault on *all* women's reproductive rights, as are the proposals in various state legislatures to force Norplant contraception or to sterilize welfare mothers. Recently battered women's service groups have also included welfare mothers in their political action, since so many of the mothers have left battering men. (Some say as many as 60%.)

Myths and stereotypes

It is the means-tested "recipients" who are stigmatized. The media are willing accomplices of business interests and public officials in stereotyping "welfare moms." The general public is abysmally ignorant about welfare. Myths abound. Mimi Abramovitz, author of *Regulating the Lives of Women*, debunks some of them, as follows:

• Women on welfare have an average of two children, slightly less than the size of the average family in the U.S.

• The average welfare benefit nationwide is $367 a month or $4,400 a year. This is almost $9,000 less than the federal poverty line for a family of three.

• Contrary to the belief that welfare mothers don't work, more than half of women on welfare stay on the rolls for less than one year. A quarter leave within four months, and only one-third stay more than two years. Yet many return to the rolls because their jobs don't pay enough to support their families.

• Almost half use welfare as a form of unemployment benefits between jobs or when they first enter the labor market, one-fifth work at such low-wage jobs that they continue to qualify for welfare, and nearly one-fifth use welfare as temporary disability insurance.

• Of the 13 million AFDC recipients, only 4 million are adults, 90% of whom are women—many, mothers of young children. In more than half of welfare homes, the youngest child is under 5 years of age. Many adult women on welfare are not able to work due to illness, disability or lack of education and job skills.

• Contrary to the belief that women on welfare have "kids for money," studies have found no link between the AFDC grant and births outside of marriage. Those births are no more frequent in high benefit states and no greater in states with rising grant levels than in states with flat or falling AFDC payments. In Mississippi, for example, the illegitimacy rate is higher than in Vermont, despite the fact that grants levels in Mississippi are much lower. States provide between $40 and $65 a month per additional child— not a very attractive bonus for such a tough job as raising a child.

• AFDC costs only 1% of the federal budget and 3.4% of the average state budget. The federal and state governments together spent $23 billion on welfare in 1991.

• Mandatory programs such as workfare do not work very well, and are expensive. The best way to encourage AFDC parents to go to work is to expand the economy and pay high enough wages to support a family. Then, people go to work if they can. The most highly touted workfare program, the GAIN [Greater Avenues for Independence] program in California, showed that workfare participants averaged only $1,901 in annual earned income. Participants earned an average of $271 more per year than non-participants and received $281 a year less in welfare. A University of Wisconsin study found that Learnfare (the program which docks up to $200 a month from a welfare mother's check if her children miss school without an acceptable excuse) failed to improve the school attendance of welfare children, but did exacerbate pre-existing family problems.

Many of the features of the PRA have already been put into practice by the states, with the help of the Clinton Administration. Donna Shalala, Secretary of Health and Human Services, has granted states many waivers from AFDC federal regulations to conduct "experiments" on recipients. These include a "Learnfare" program in Wisconsin that cuts AFDC grants when a child misses school a certain number of times; workfare programs in various states; "shotfare" programs that cut the grant if a mother does not get her child immunized; and "family cap" programs that refuse benefits for a child born after mother is on AFDC. Massachusetts asked for permission to implement certain aspects of its recently passed law, including putting a two-year time limit on AFDC grants. Lawyers sued the state on the ground that these "experiments" violate the intent of federal AFDC law, which allows genuine experimentation to test a program on a small scale with the goal of improving it. The state proposals are not real experiments since they are applied wholesale to the entire AFDC population without any control group and, lawyers argued, they violate the rights of human subjects.

Disciplining the work force

In their book, *Regulating the Poor*, Frances Fox Piven and Richard Cloward make a convincing argument for the thesis that welfare expands during times of civil turmoil, as during the Depression and the 1960s, in order to quell the turmoil, and contracts after the turmoil has subsided in order to discipline the work force. Income maintenance programs lessen economic insecurity, thus weakening capital's ability to depress wages. According to a principle in social welfare theory called "the principle of less eligibility," welfare pays lower than the lowest paid wages, in order to make *any* kind of work at *any* wage more desirable than welfare. However, that principle was challenged in the early 1970s when unemployment rose to the highest levels since the 1930s, and wages did not fall. Welfare benefits were sometimes competitive with wages during that period. Employers concluded that the expansion of income maintenance programs in the late 1960s and early 1970s had insulated wages from the effects of rising unemployment. They pressured legislators to slash benefits to remove the safety net that made it possible for people to avoid low-wage jobs. AFDC grant levels continued to fall until now they are only about half of the official poverty level in a majority of states, and less than a third of that level in a quarter of the states. And the poverty level is itself a very inadequate index of poverty.

Unemployment insurance has also been slashed. Although originally tax-exempt, it became fully taxable during the 1980s. When the unemployment level required to trigger benefits was raised, fewer people received benefits beyond the basic 26 weeks. The number of workers who have exhausted their benefits is higher than at any time since 1951, when they began collecting data on the program.

The repeal of the Comprehensive Education and Training Act removed 400,000 people from public service jobs. Disability rolls were slashed from both the Supplemental Security Income (SSI) and Social Security Disability (SSDI) rolls. The Food Stamp program introduced various rules that cut people from the rolls, including work registration requirements and making strikers ineligible.

Stigmatizing welfare recipients is a form of terrorism to frighten the entire population off the rolls.

Piven and Cloward point out that the expanding service sector of the economy relies on a new "service proletariat" of low-wage workers, the vast majority of whom are women and minorities, who cook, serve, and clean. The attack on social programs occurred at the same time as increasingly large numbers of women entered the labor market. Cutting back programs that supplement their wages such as health benefits and Food Stamps makes them even more vulnerable in the job market.

Stigmatizing welfare recipients is a form of terrorism to frighten the entire population off the rolls. If people can be made to believe that welfare recipients are a lower form of humanity, they will go to great lengths to avoid becoming members of that degraded population. The scapegoating takes on racial dimensions when the majority of women and children on AFDC are blacks and Hispanics (40% black and 16% Hispanic in 1992). Piven and Cloward point out that the post–World War II black movement was largely responsible for creating the political pressures which led to the expansion of social spending in the 1960s. The current cutbacks are part of a racist backlash by whites against the rights that blacks gained in the 1960s.

Where are the jobs?

Conservative social scientists propose to dismantle the welfare state; liberal ones tinker with it. But both the liberals and conservatives are preoccupied with getting AFDC mothers into the work force. A liberal proposal that has been getting some attention recently, including an article in the *Nation*, was proposed by economists Barbara Bergmann and Heidi Hartmann, Co-chairs of the Economists' Policy Group for Women's Issues. They say that AFDC mothers could work and support their families, even with minimum wage jobs, if they were provided with health care, child care, Earned Income Tax Credit, Food Stamps, and housing assistance. But they minimize the difficulty of finding jobs and exaggerate the level of job skills of AFDC mothers. They claim that most AFDC recipients have a high school diploma, when in fact over one-half do not. In the last 20 years, the incomes of high school dropouts entering the work force have plummeted 41%.

Compared to other single mothers, AFDC mothers are not only less educated, but also younger, have younger children, and are more likely to be African-American or Latina—all factors leading to lower earnings potential. Young workers have faced deteriorating employment prospects and lower earnings in recent years.

Bergmann and Hartmann recommend education and training, but they make no mention of the importance of a college education in these days of high unemployment. While a college education offers no guarantees, without it women will surely be tracked into the low-wage female sector of the work force.

Bergmann and Hartmann do not call for raising the minimum wage, even though that would be the single most effective way to raise workers out of poverty. Although the Earned Income Tax Credit helps to raise a minimum wage, it is in fact a subsidy to employers. Why let them off the hook by subsidizing their low wages, rather than forcing them to pay better wages? And, although Food Stamps are a life saver to many families, they are also a means to subsidize agribusiness and food corporations. Furthermore, those who use them are subjected to humiliating ceremonies every time they buy groceries. Why not give people cash to buy their food, either in the form of wages or adequate welfare grants?

Bergmann and Hartmann do not support the right of a mother (or father) to care for young children themselves rather than putting the children into day care. Many women (and probably some men) would prefer to stay home to care for their children. In fact, a 1992 Roper poll showed that to be a majority opinion, with 53 percent of all women and 64 percent of married women in the United States saying that they preferred to stay at home. Only a third of married women worked full-time throughout the year in 1992, and only 23 percent of them had children under the age of three, even though they had a male partner to help juggle earner-parent roles.

Or is the right to care for your own children at home to be reserved for two-parent affluent families and not single welfare mothers burdened with working and caring for children, without the help of a partner? Even David Ellwood, Clinton's welfare advisor, concedes that single parents of young children should not be expected to work full-time since they are doubly burdened by work and child care. And part-time work usually does not even support a single person, let alone a family.

Because of their child care responsibilities, women with children work for wages considerably fewer hours than women without children. In their book, *Glass Ceilings and Bottomless Pits*, Randy Albelda and Chris Tilly point out that in 1991 in Massachusetts, single women with children worked an average of 908 hours a year while single women without children worked an average of 1,423 hours a year. (A year-round, full-time job typically is 2,000 hours per year.) And after their waged job, they have two other full-time jobs. Even when mothers put their children in child care, they spend "an average of 37 hours a week taking care of children—another full-time job." And household work amounts to another full-time job—50 hours a week, according to one estimate.

Many European countries do not view single mothers as a "problem." In fact, in Britain single mothers are expected to stay at home with their children and be supported by the public if they are in financial need. In Norway, about 70% of all single mothers with children under age 10 receive a Transitional Benefit Program which is indexed and tax-free, and is worth about two-thirds of the wages of the average female worker. All of the Nordic countries (Norway, Sweden, Denmark, Finland, and Iceland) have established some form of guaranteed child support payment, paid for by the government when non-custodial parents fail to pay or pay inadequately.

Assuming that the mother has child care, health insurance, and housing subsidy in place and is ready to go to work—where are the jobs? The National Jobs for All Coalition points out that although the U.S. does not regularly collect job vacancy data, "the occasional surveys of jobs vacancies show that even when unemployment rates are much lower than the current national average, there are several times as many job seekers as available jobs." One study in Harlem, New York, found that 14 people applied for every job opening in fast food restaurants during a five-month period in early 1993. Among those who were rejected, 73% had not found work of any kind a year later. The younger applicants, especially those under 20, had the most trouble finding a job.

Wall Street quakes when unemployment drops. The Federal Reserve bank raises interest rates whenever unemployment dips below six percent, keeping 18 million Americans either fully or partially unemployed. As the National Jobs for All Coalition puts it, "The unemployed are, in effect, involuntary 'inflation fighters,' drafted to hold down wages and prices." What will happen when millions of AFDC mothers enter an already depressed labor market?

Guaranteed income

Economists and policy makers are speculating about the permanent loss of jobs due in part to technology. There are many different points of view about this. The National Jobs for All Coalition calls for creating jobs in order to have full employment ("Fair Work, instead of Workfare"). On the other hand, Stanley Aronowitz and William DiFazio say in their book, *The Jobless Future*, that large-scale unemployment is a permanent feature of the economy and we therefore need a guaranteed annual income. A proposal called the Basic Income Grant, a form of guaranteed annual income, is being seriously considered in Europe.

The French political philosopher, André Gorz, argues for *both* guaranteed work and guaranteed income. He fears that a guaranteed income without guaranteed work is fundamentally flawed because it leads to a dual stratification of society, consolidating a system dominated by capitalist relations of production and by what he calls the "working elite." The guaranteed minimum, he says, is a way of accepting this split-up and making it more tolerable. Gorz advocates distributing the labor savings brought about by technological changes in such a way that everyone can work, but work less without losing income. In his plan, there would be less work but greater flexibility of work time—perhaps a total of 20,000 hours of work over a lifetime which could be divided up in many ways— "ten years of full-time work, or twenty years of half-time work; or—a more likely and sensible choice—forty years of intermittent work." Regrettably, Gorz categorizes caretaking as a "spare time" activity in between intermittent work periods, when it should be regarded as paid work, and hard work at that.

I prefer Gorz's approach to the problem, but regardless of where one stands in this debate, everyone agrees that the labor market as it now exists cannot serve the needs of most workers. One should not, of course, accept the dominant capitalist view of how much "necessary work" there is. There is a vast amount of socially necessary work that needs to be done to meet presently unmet human needs. Caretaking is one of those important jobs. It seems ironic that in an era when jobs are disappearing forever, policymakers should be so eager to force single mothers into the waged work force. We should instead be placing a greater value on caretaking and providing decent remuneration for it.

Many European countries do not view single mothers as a "problem."

Bergmann and Hartmann propose a fall-back package for unemployed parents, consisting mostly of vouchers for necessities. But here their distrust of the poor rears its ugly head. Since welfare began, there have always been policymakers who believed that the poor could not be trusted to spend their own money and needed supervision. Where is their evidence that they are not capable of spending their money wisely? The poor correctly perceive vouchers as an insult.

The Family Support Act of 1988 called for requiring waged work of welfare recipients, but it also called for the supports to make this possible, including child care and health insurance. Many policymakers agreed with the work requirement, arguing that the supports would enable welfare recipients to get a waged job. However, it did not work out. Proposals for health insurance were killed. Child care subsidies were increased only slightly. Subsidized housing was cut back. The realities of recession and conservatism took over and the welfare "reform" which some people thought held much promise became merely another punitive law making life more difficult for poor mothers.

Reformers can concoct schemes that look good on paper, but they would do better to put their energy into saving the essential programs that exist, weak though they are. The Republicans' proposal for ending AFDC as an entitlement program and turning it over to the states in a block grant would tear apart the meager safety net that exists for poor mothers and children. The first order of business is to save AFDC as a federalized program and improve it, raising the grants to at least the poverty level. After we do that, we can begin the long hard road to win universal health insurance and universal day care. After that, perhaps we can begin to work for a guaranteed annual income or, at the very least, a universal family allowance. Whatever we work for, it should be universal and not means-tested.

The first order of business is to save AFDC as a federalized program and improve it.

The only good thing about the Contract With America is that it frightened a lot of people into an awareness that legislators are increasingly becoming the lackeys of the avaricious and powerful rich. It has the potential for uniting people on the left who had previously been working on single issues, and it has inspired a new spirit of activism.

The National Welfare Rights Organization (NWRO) died in the early 1970s, and there was no large-scale national welfare organizing until the formation of the National Welfare Rights Union (NWRU) in 1987. It was formed by people from various advocacy groups. It has chapters in several states and holds national board meetings and conferences. The president, Marian Kramer, has been one of the main speakers at NOW marches and is frequently called upon to speak by other organizations. Many of its members and allies are veterans of the NWRO movement.

Welfare organizing continued in some states even after the demise of the NWRO. Massachusetts has a particularly strong network of welfare organizing and advocacy which includes a state-wide organization of welfare mothers, the Coalition for Basic Human Needs, and Massachusetts Welfare Rights Union, as well as several advocacy groups working on welfare issues. Two University of Massachusetts professors, Ann Withorn and Randy Albelda, organized about 100 academics into a group called Academic Working Group on Poverty. Its members are popularizing welfare information for the general public. In cooperation with *Survival News*, a newspaper for and by low-income people which I founded in 1987, they are setting up a speakers' and consultants' bureau. They are also doing research requested by Massachusetts Law Reform to help in a suit against the state regarding waivers.[1]

The failure of the left

The old left has, for the most part, been conspicuously absent from the welfare debate until recently, and while the new left has considered it in their theoretical works, they have not put welfare struggles very high on their agenda. The reasons for the absence of the old left may be similar to the reasons of the men who constructed the first social insurance program in this country. They responded to the demands of an elite, largely male, white working class and did not ally themselves with married mothers in their role as caretakers, single working mothers, domestic workers, or black sharecroppers.

Radicals have always been ambivalent about the welfare state, ever since the German Chancellor Otto von Bismarck gave pensions to state workers to "silence the siren sounds of Socialism." Welfare is often used for social control and to stave off more radical reform. It has often bought off militants at a very low price. Yet it has also been fought for by workers, parents, and students. The United Nations Declaration of Human Rights asserts that people have a right to have their basic needs met. Although the United States never signed that declaration, we are *entitled* to a guarantee that our basic needs will be met, and we are *entitled* to have a voice in how our welfare state will be run.

Newt Gingrich professes to admire Thomas Jefferson, but has he read his 1785 letter to James Madison in which he warns against an inequity of wealth? "The consequences of this enormous inequality (in France) producing so much misery to the bulk of mankind, legislators cannot invent too many devices for subdividing property." As an Enlightenment man, Jefferson argued for a more equitable distribution of wealth with reasons based not on morality, but on self-interest. The French Revolution was only four years away.

Gingrich considers himself a futurist. Can he, or anyone else, imagine what our country will look like in four years if he and his like continue to turn their back on the poor? Who among the right will be the Robert McNamara [U.S. defense secretary, 1961–1968] to come forth then and weep tears of contrition for homeless bands of starving people?

Notes

1. For a fuller discussion of the history of welfare organizing in Massachusetts, see Betty Reid Mandell and Ann Withorn, "Keep on Keeping On: Organizing for Welfare Rights in Massachusetts"; in Robert Fisher and Joseph Kling, Eds., *Mobilizing the Community: Local Politics in the Era of the Global City*. Newbury Park, CA: Sage, 1993.

2

Welfare Reform Is a Mistake

The Women's Alliance

The Women's Alliance is a community group in Framingham, Massachusetts, that assists low-income women in such areas as child care, housing, and welfare.

Welfare-reform programs similar to those in Massachusetts will unjustly punish welfare recipients by cutting off benefits after two years. To keep their benefits, individuals would be forced to work. However, programs that mandate work have failed to improve the employability of participants. Workfare programs also cost taxpayers more money to administer than is saved by reducing the number of welfare recipients. Government must recognize that child care is important and valuable work and that unemployed single mothers should not be penalized for staying home to raise their children.

Welfare recipients have become the disenfranchised group most fashionable for candidates (not only on the Right!) to use for political capital. Because they are already hated by many, heavily stereotyped, and have little political voice, they are easy targets. The Women's Alliance, whose members include women with low wage jobs, or who are on welfare or disability insurance, is asking for your active help in dispelling the lies at this crucial time of legislative "change" on welfare issues.

As part of this viewpoint, we offer a number of voices addressing the issue of so-called welfare reform. Grace Ross, staff person of the Women's Alliance, wrote the introduction and postscript; Lisa Sanderson, a mother of one (who ended up on welfare when she became pregnant, after working full-time outside of the home since she was fourteen) writes about key problems with the welfare proposals; Lauretta Billingsley, not herself a mother or on welfare, but a concerned citizen, shares her conviction that welfare issues are relevant to all women; Maureen Gomes writes from the perspective of a formerly battered woman; and Loretta Crowley, also a mother on welfare, discusses making the sacrifice to go on welfare for the sake of her child, and the moral poverty of those unwilling to help each other out, and the next generation as well.

Women's Alliance, "End Poverty as We Know It (Not Welfare!)," *Resist*, May/June 1994. This article is reprinted with permission from *Resist*. *Resist* has been funding social change since 1967.

GRACE ROSS: "Welfare Reform" is becoming a rallying cry at both local and national levels of government. Despite the rhetoric, this discussion has not been about how we should support those in our society who need it most to get out of poverty, nor about how to restructure our economy to support single-parent families. The dismantling of the welfare system in Massachusetts is serving as a prototype for the Clinton administration to focus the disgruntled and frustrated middle and working class on "those lazy bums" "stealing" from the taxpayers (although the amount of tax money poured into the Savings and Loan bail-out would pay for all welfare in the United States for five years!).

Workfare does not "provide recipients with valuable work experience"; studies show it does not increase long-term employability at all.

Punitive proposals in Massachusetts have taken form under the leadership of Republican Gov. William Weld and Sen. Therese Murray (D-Plymouth), who has been wooed by the "new democrats" in Washington. Weld's proposal includes a complete end to AFDC [Aid to Families with Dependent Children], replacing it with workfare—recipients would be forced to work full time to receive benefits, or be cut off entirely. Sen. Murray's proposal would allow: recipients to go to school or get job training (as welfare presently offers); or, an employer subsidy program in which grants would be paid to employers to hire recipients—the employer would put $1/hour into a fund made available to the recipient only after a year; or workfare for a little over half time; or no welfare.

A number of proposals include a two-year time limit on all benefits, whether or not a recipient does workfare or is trying to finish an educational program. Another proposal, partially written by recipients themselves, would supply extended Medicaid and childcare subsidies for those recipients ready to take a "paying job." [As of August 1996, these two proposals had not been enacted.] National proposals are not yet specific but many will be similar to those under discussion here in Massachusetts.

The principle argument for punitive welfare reform is that people who receive benefits are costing the taxpayers money. Nationally, welfare makes up less than two cents of every tax dollar; in Massachusetts, about three cents actually goes to recipients. Both of these figures are dwarfed by the amount of tax dollars not collected from corporations and the very rich through special tax deductions. The other arguments we hear are also based on misinformation—that welfare recipients are lazy drug addicts who don't work. Parenting *is* work, especially when you do it alone with no breaks. And finally the "argument" that jobs (as opposed to welfare) improve self-esteem not only ignores the work of parenting, and the punitive nature of some jobs, but misses the fact that the worst blow to recipients' self-esteem is prejudice.

And watch the rhetoric. Forcing recipients to find jobs assumes there *are* paid jobs out there. Forcing recipients to do community service treats them like criminals, and has nothing to do with "at least volunteering if they cannot find work"; this is not volunteering, this is indentured servitude. *And it cost taxpayers more money in every state it has been tried.* Workfare does not "provide recipients with valuable work experience"; studies show it does not increase long-term employability at all.

Every new regulatory program "for" the poor costs more money in bureaucracy than it saves, and creates more human suffering. Welfare recipients, like the members of any social group, make the best choices for their families among the options available.

Perhaps the worst idea is that of "time limited benefits." Why? The proposed two-year time limit comes from the fact that most recipients are only on welfare for two years or less, according to statistics gathered in the late eighties (i.e. when we were not in a recession). But many end up going back to welfare if they have daycare problems, or no medical insurance, and their children get sick.

More importantly, those who have hidden illnesses (such as chronic fatigue and other diseases not recognized by disability insurance), those whose children have chronic behavior, health, or learning problems, or women who need more education in order to get a job that can support their families, will end up homeless and in the street. That result will be incredibly expensive for taxpayers—not to mention the moral costs to all of us.

The final straw is the work program supported by Sen. Murray. Given the barriers welfare recipients face in finding and keeping a job, some kind of incentive to employers might make sense. But Sen. Murray's idea is to remove a subsidy from the poor (whom we know need it) and give it to companies who have already received significant tax breaks from Gov. Weld at taxpayers' expense. Three-fourths of Massachusetts corporations pay the minimum corporate tax—around $500 per year, which is less than the average individual!

Sen. Murray's plan is to take a recipient's welfare check and food stamps, and pay them to an employer. The employer then pays them back to the recipient in exchange for forty hours of work a week; the employer is only expected to pay $1/hour into an account that the recipient can only get access to at the end of the year. If an employer can get a worker for a dollar an hour instead of someone else at minimum wage, taxpayers will have to pay twice: once to the employer for the recipient and a second time for the unemployment check for the ex-worker. Recipients will have no regular rights as workers, and will have to accept whatever treatment they get for an entire year just to see some benefits from their labor (those saved up dollars!—and who gets them if the recipient, conveniently, does not finish out the year?)

This program makes no sense—it costs jobs, spends taxpayer money, sets recipients up as indentured servants, and undercuts the wage scale and workers' rights.

Other bad stuff to watch out for?

LISA SANDERSON:
• *Fingerprints for welfare cards.* They want to fingerprint us, like common criminals. We are not the criminals in this case, the deadbeat dads are. Why not fingerprint them?
• *Emergency Assistance and Vendor Payment Rent.* If you use your emergency assistance in the previous year to pay your rent, they want to auto-

matically deduct your rent from your check and pay it directly to your landlord. In other words, they're saying we are irresponsible parents who don't know how to manage our money. The real problem is we are 45% to 55% below the poverty level and don't have enough money to manage!

• *Welfare records being made public.* This would mean that anyone can see our welfare records and figure out where we are and how much we get. A study done on Cape Cod found that 50% of women on AFDC left battering situations. Opening our records would mean batterers could find us and harm and/or kill our children and ourselves.

• *Learnfare.* If your child missed more than 15 days of school in a year, they would cut your welfare. This is ridiculous. Lots of children miss that many days for legitimate reasons but learnfare doesn't allow exceptions.

• *No exemption for mothers with young children.* Even though a Carnegie Foundation study released in April 1994 showed the importance of parenting in the first few years of a child's life, and even though federal law supposedly protects us—the Murray bill does not exempt single parents of children aged three and under from having to do workfare or take a full-time job—this one is going to be a big battle!

Women must stand together

LAURETTA BILLINGSLEY: In 1994, the Women's Alliance co-sponsored a forum on welfare reform at the University of Massachusetts in Boston. I was really fired up to be part of this group. Sarah Ann Shaw of Channel 4 was the moderator. The other panelists were Renae Scott of The Women's Theological Center; Ann Withorn, faculty member at the College of Public and Community Service; Dottie Stevens of The National Welfare Rights Union; Sen. Dianne Wilkerson; and Ellen Convisser of the National Organization for Women. Sarah Ann Shaw was more than a moderator; she has been working on women's issues for about 30 years.

This was a breakthrough meeting! Women from many classes and races, and with diverse agendas, stood up to say they recognize this so called "welfare reform" as punitive and as "an attack on all women." NOW has made working on this issue part of their national agenda. Senator Wilkerson made it clear that to this point there has been no support from a broad range of women's groups, and she encouraged groups to get on board now as the welfare reform bills are being debated. Wilkerson, Withorn and others stressed the point that women with and without jobs have many similar problems, particularly the need for good childcare, and childcare when a child is sick, which is not addressed adequately by pending legislation. The mixed signals sent by our society were examined in light of the decreased budget for daycare at the Massachusetts Office for Children. Weld says he will provide daycare for the children of the 50,000 families he's pushing off AFDC, but the 1995 budget does not reflect funding for even 5 additional daycare slots.

Jobs for the 50,000 families pushed off AFDC is another bailiwick. These folks will have to get in line behind the 200,000 people who received unemployment in February 1994. Welfare reform without job creation is just putting women and children in back alleys to die. I believe the legislators know this but do not want the public to have time to clearly see the state of affairs in the Commonwealth and the nation. Lack of money, always pointed out when it comes to welfare, is never an issue when there is an "entitlement" for businesses like the Massachusetts industry incentive that cost $72 million. How about tying state business "welfare" to job creation for the AFDC recipients on whose backs Weld is trying to build his career?

Our economic system simply does not allow women to have children and enough money and time to raise them.

Weld and other politicians can enact these kind of policies, in part, because women themselves are not clear about where we stand on this issue. Our economic system simply does not allow women to have children and enough money and time to raise them, whether they have an outside paying job or not. Until women realize we all rise together or sink together, and pledge their support to disadvantaged women, the battle cannot be won. I struggled myself with understanding the circumstances that women face when receiving AFDC. Working in the trenches and still not being totally clear, I can only imagine that for professional women who do not personally know women on AFDC and their challenges, all this must seem distant and incomprehensible. The only possible way to develop a progressive, enlightened social policy is for women, both workers and mothers, to stand together.

More than 50% run from batterers

Maureen E. Gomes: I am one of the many welfare mothers whose only escape out of battering was to end up on welfare. I became homeless in 1989 when I became pregnant with my daughter and my mother refused to keep us. Upon entering into my first apartment, I felt relieved; I had a home for Ashley. At 18, I met a man who became the father of my son, and I thought things were going to work out.

Then the abuse started. For a little more than a year I was brutally beaten and abused. I finally decided to leave the situation. He retaliated by trashing the whole apartment along with everything I owned. I went back to salvage what I could and he returned trying to strangle me—only his sister's unexpected appearance saved me and I was able to get away. I was left with an eviction notice, having to move, $850 worth of damages, and many nightmares.

Now I am alone with two children. I have an MRVP certificate (a state housing subsidy) that has been cut so much that I now pay more than half my income in rent. My rent keeps going up and it is becoming impossible to pay all of the expenses and clothe my children and myself with this small income. For the time being I feel pretty safe. My son's father is in jail for an attempted murder on someone else.

Everyone knows he will be paroled someday. He is up for parole now and I am collecting letters and trying to keep him in jail. If I fail or if he gets out later, several problems with both welfare and the changes in the MRVP program could make me one of those gruesome statistics.

The continued loss in income for AFDC recipients as inflation goes up, and the cuts in the MRVP program, are already problem enough for all of us on AFDC and MRVP—not enough food, etc. But what will happen for battered women? What if we can no longer afford our telephone? Not just for medical emergencies for our children, but what if my batterer starts trying to break down the door and I cannot call the police?

What about his having trashed my apartment once already? What if he does it again? What if I lose my housing certificate? There is no last month's rent and security deposit anymore with MRVP. If I have to move suddenly, it would take many months to save enough or raise enough money to move. In my last place, the lack of money for inspections and administration of the program meant that I finally left because I could not get my window locks fixed on my basement apartment.

Welfare reform is confusing; welfare bashing is not

LORETTA CROWLEY: I was not sure what welfare reform really meant until I went to a hearing. I was surprised about how much insight there was into the situations of welfare recipients. Everyone there brought up new ways of looking at it.

One senator talked at length about fraud. I felt the legislators on the panel stood up for us—one woman senator brought up the fact that there was fraud in other businesses, not even comparable to welfare fraud because it was so much more.

> *It has made me mad to listen to the different government speakers because they clearly have not bothered to listen to AFDC recipients.*

I really appreciate hard work, but it should be voluntary. A man said, "I see nothing wrong with community service." Neither do I, but we all go through crises in our lives and recovery is unique to each individual. I don't know what forcing someone to do community service might do to their mental health. It is not just a question of able-bodied, it is a question of able-minded too. I am sure that those who are ready will volunteer, but it needs to be the individual's choice.

I agreed with the doctor who came to testify, the head of pediatrics from Boston City Hospital. He talked about the importance of bonding between parents and our children, the importance of raising our own children and the importance of staying home with our kids.

From a Christian point of view, I would not bash welfare recipients or I would be a hypocrite—what became of the capability and obligation of people to give emotional support without judgement?

I see poverty as an attitude held by those who do not care or are unwilling to support their neighbors, not as our problem just because we are short on money. A lot of us have worked and paid taxes, and we all have families who are paying into the system as well. Some people think it is their money that is used to help welfare recipients without considering that we have put money into the tax system also.

If people in power want to keep people in poverty, I still feel working to raise one's children should be a choice. Even though we are 45% to 55% below the poverty level, it is a sacrifice that we make because our priority is to be with our children. When I hear a political leader like Gov. Weld say to just cut welfare off, I think "how civilized." Now that attitude is poverty!

Government bashes AFDC recipients

LISA SANDERSON: It has made me mad to listen to the different government speakers because they clearly have not bothered to listen to AFDC recipients, even though there was a series of state hearings across the state. They refuse to acknowledge that being a single parent is a full-time job—although they do if they have to hire a childcare provider for us while we go to work! They want to force us into minimum wage jobs, generally less than they will have to pay for a childcare provider! My sister Kim has called every childcare place she can find and they all want over $100 per week and will not even take her son because Matthew is less than two and a half years old. What will they do for children like mine who are 15 months old?

The director of the Athol Community Development Corporation has talked at length about how bad it is for your self-esteem and self-respect to be unemployed and sitting around at home all the time not doing anything; he said that was his experience of being unemployed. He must not have a child (at least not alone) because I don't find I have time to sit around watching soap operas and eating bonbons all day.

I must have spent a few days asking everyone I knew how their self-esteem and self-respect were going. My comparison between folks out on the job and us at home (on the job) was not noticeably different. He clearly has not had jobs where he was treated really badly all the time like many of us. My sense of responsibility and self-esteem is a hundred percent more since I have been a mother than for the eleven years before that when I worked forty hours per week.

I wonder why they think childcare providers are better for our children than we are? What about the added costs when you take an outside job—for work clothes, supply of diapers, wipes, etc. for the childcare place, and for transportation to get back and forth to work and the childcare place? And what about sick leave, well appointments, etc. for your child as well as yourself?

Our responsibility as a civilized society is the end of POVERTY as we know it, not the end of welfare.

I was struck by one woman's story of having to leave her husband when he tried to force feed their child her vomit after she threw up at the dinner table. How many of us come from battering situations or abusive homes and ended up on welfare? Then we get battered by the welfare system. I am really tired of having to get up and fight to show it is important for me to stay home with my child and that parenting is work. Why is it okay in a two-parent family for a mother to stay home without any questions but not me?

GRACE ROSS: The Pope and the Canadian Government came out publicly in support of paying women for the work they do raising children—something that women activists have been fighting for for a long time. But just like in these cases, the Massachusetts and U.S. governments are behind most developed countries.

Statistics show one in four children in the U.S. live in poverty part of their lives. Our responsibility as a civilized society is the end of POVERTY as we know it, not the end of welfare. Initiatives like universal healthcare, increased minimum wage (up to the poverty level!), decent and affordable daycare for all (like in many European countries), a family stipend (like in many European countries) and pay for women's work raising children (like the Canadian government has at least recognized the need for) would go a long way to getting not only welfare recipients, but all families, out of poverty. And it would give dignity to all.

3

Welfare Reform Violates Women's Rights

Mimi Abramovitz

Mimi Abramovitz is a professor of social policy at the Hunter College of Social Work in New York City and is the author of Under Attack, Fighting Back: Women and Welfare in the U.S.

Welfare reform has become a mean-spirited campaign to modify poor women's behavior and deny them their rights. This effort vilifies the marital, childbearing, and parenting behavior of poor women. Welfare reformers falsely portray recipients as "welfare queens" who prefer welfare to work, lie to gain benefits, and have additional children in order to get more aid. In actuality, cutting welfare benefits and forcing women to work will make it more difficult for them to raise and support their children. Welfare advocates and the poor must organize to prevent such punitive welfare policies.

Frances Fox Piven wrote in *Democratic Left* in 1994 about the faulty assumptions and cruel logic of the Clinton administration's welfare reform proposals. No one could have guessed then just how far and how fast the public debate on welfare would swing to the right. As I write today (in mid-April 1995), the Republicans' "Personal Responsibility Act," which is even more punitive than Bill Clinton's "Work and Personal Responsibility Act," has passed the House and awaits consideration in the Senate. Even if Clinton vetoes this first bill [he did so in January 1996], it's almost certain that some kind of regressive welfare "reform" will become law before the 1996 elections. Welfare reform is bad for women, because they are the direct target of a drive to modify women's behavior; bad for children, who will see less of their mothers; bad for labor, who will face more competition for fewer jobs; bad for the poor, because it makes them poorer; and bad for the middle class, because their programs are next.

So we on the left have our work cut out for us. Just as the right patiently laid the groundwork over twenty years for its assault on the

Mimi Abramovitz, "Welfare and Women's Lives." This article originally appeared in the May/June 1995 issue of *Democratic Left*, published by the Democratic Socialists of America. It is reprinted here by permission.

public sector, we need to do the slow work of building cohesive movements for social justice. A crucial part of this work will be raising public consciousness of welfare as a feminist issue—not just in the superficial sense that most welfare recipients are women, but also with the understanding that the availability of welfare affects *all* women's ability to resist sexist workplaces and family structures.

Welfare reform has turned into a mean-spirited campaign to modify women's behavior and dismantle the welfare state. When Aid to Families With Dependent Children (AFDC) was created in 1935, Congress's intention was to cushion poverty and to enable mothers to stay home with their kids. AFDC has never performed either of these functions well, and feminists and the left have criticized it for years.

But now things have gone from bad to worse. Instead of fixing AFDC to compensate for the falling standard of living, the new welfare reform deflects attention from the sagging economy by maligning the marital, childbearing, and parenting behavior of poor women. To build support for their plans, the welfare cutters evoke false stereotypes of recipients as culturally adrift welfare queens who prefer welfare to work, live high on the hog, cheat the government, and have kids for money. The rhetoric of this assault is highly racialized. Although 40 percent of the welfare caseload nationwide is white, the reformers do not hesitate to pander to white voters' worst instincts. Richard Nixon had his "southern strategy," Ronald Reagan had his welfare queen, George Bush had Willie Horton [a convicted murderer featured in Bush political ads], and today's politicians have welfare reform.

Targets of welfare reform

The first target of welfare reform is women's work behavior. Time limits and workfare plans presume that women do not want to work and need to be coerced into the labor market. But in fact, 70 percent of all AFDC recipients do leave the rolls within two years for work or marriage. A significant number of these women return within five years because of unstable jobs, failed relationships, or the lack of child care and health benefits. The remaining 30 percent are people who cannot compete effectively in today's labor market because of lack of education and skills, illness, disability, or emotional problems. They need supportive services, not punitive reforms.

The push for mandatory work requirements also ignores years of research showing that welfare-to-work programs have only modest results. This is not terribly surprising. First, there are not enough jobs for all those willing and able to work—and the Federal Reserve works hard to keep things that way. Second, the low-paying, part-time jobs available to poor women lack benefits and union protection. Given these conditions, the administration's promise "to make work pay for those who try hard and play by the rules" rings hollow for welfare mothers. It also devalues their work at home. Finally, cutting welfare means the loss of many public sector jobs, which for years have provided large numbers of white women and women of color a way out of poverty.

The second target of welfare reform, women's childbearing behavior, challenges women's reproductive rights. Both parties have expanded the child exclusion provision, which denies aid to children born on AFDC, and stiffened paternity procedures. These changes imply that women on welfare have large families, when in fact the average family on welfare is a mother and two children, the same as the rest of us. Forty-three percent of AFDC families have one child and 30 percent have two. Since you have to have at least one child to qualify for AFDC, this means that most women have just one additional child while on the rolls. It also suggests that women on welfare do not have children for money. But 76 researchers recently announced that there is no evidence for a link between the availability of welfare and a woman's childbearing decisions.

Welfare is an issue for women because politicians have built support for their attack on women's rights by blaming all women for the nation's woes.

The Republicans have made controlling women's reproductive choices the main goal of welfare reform. The stated purpose of their bill is to put an end to "illegitimacy." They say mother-only families—encouraged by welfare—have produced drug dealers, drive-by shooters, and the deficit. To end "illegitimacy," they plan a range of horrific child exclusion provisions, some denying aid to children and young unwed mothers forever. The Republican paternity procedures hold back AFDC until the state establishes paternity, which can take months, leaving even more women out in the cold. If the pregnancies persist despite these penalties, the Republicans tell mothers to turn to relatives, apply for private charity, or place their children in "orphanages."

Although only 8 percent of all AFDC households are headed by teens, the welfare reformers pander to public worries about "babies having babies." If preventing teen pregnancy were the real goal of welfare reform, we would hear more about sex education, family planning, abortion services, and awareness of the complexities of teen pregnancy.

The third target of welfare reform is the parenting behavior of poor women and men. The welfare reform debate displays a deep distrust of parenting by poor women. Supporters of "orphanages" publicly suggest that any caretaking is better than that provided by welfare mothers, even though many have hired poor women in their own homes.

In the name of promoting parental responsibility, welfare reform forces single mothers to work, shrinks the AFDC check, and otherwise undercuts the conditions for effective parenting. Forcing women to work makes it harder for mothers to supervise their children. This makes little sense, especially in neighborhoods plagued by poor schools, lack of health care, substandard housing and in some cases drugs, crime, and violence. Stricter child support enforcement clamps down on the parenting behavior of so-called "deadbeat dads." While men should be expected to support their children, welfare reform ignores that most welfare fathers are poor and unemployed, that some are already involved with their children, and that an aggressive pursuit of child support could subject women to male violence. All these efforts to enforce responsible parenting defy the research that shows that the deprivations of poverty, not the receipt of a welfare check, impair children's development on all fronts. Although the combined value of AFDC and food stamps falls below the poverty line in all fifty states, the welfare reformers are silent on raising the grant and ending poverty as we know it.

Undercutting women's gains

The current attack harms poor women and their children first and foremost for being poor. But welfare reform also fits into a broader strategy designed to take back the gains made by *all* women during the past thirty years. The proposed changes attack the rights of all women to decent pay, to control their own sexuality, to establish families free of abusive relationships, and to survive outside of the rigid family forms endorsed by the religious right. They do this by undercutting women's economic independence, weakening their caretaking supports, and threatening their reproductive rights.

Cutting AFDC benefits undercuts all women's economic independence by depriving women of a small but critical alternative to male and market income. Without this back-up many women facing hard times will have more trouble resisting an exploitative job, escaping an abusive relationship, or simply deciding to raise children alone. By forcing women to work, welfare reform twists the gains of the women's movement against poor women. Feminism has called for more choices, greater opportunities, and well-paying work for women—not coercion, workfare, and poverty-level jobs.

Welfare reform threatens the rights of all women by shifting the costs of caretaking back to the home. The attack on welfare fuels a larger attack on the nation's health, education, child care, income support, and social service programs which among other things have underwritten the cost of family maintenance and eased the caretaking burdens of middle class as well as poor women.

Welfare reform also threatens the reproductive rights of every woman. Efforts to penalize non-marital births are not far removed from the anti-abortion movement's challenge to women's reproductive choices. The foes of abortion have not yet won their battle in full. But if the government wins the right to control the bodies of poor women on welfare, it will be much easier to control the bodies of all women.

Welfare is an issue for women because politicians have built support for their attack on women's rights by blaming all women for the nation's woes. Women, welfare, and now affirmative action are being scapegoated to ease the moral panic generated by new family structures and greater economic independence among women. Welfare reform enforces traditional work and family forms by disciplining those defined as "not playing by the rules." The reformers openly hope that their stiff penalties will send a message to women about what happens to those who do not marry, who raise kids on their own, and otherwise step out of role. Since any woman can be tarred and feathered in this way, we must ask: Who made the rules? Who benefits from the rules? And can single mothers even play by a set of rules that defines their family structure as out of bounds?

While the Democrats' "Work and Personal Responsibility Act" bids for conservative votes by making welfare leaner and meaner, the Republican "Personal Responsibility Act" ups the ante by ending the welfare state altogether. It cuts welfare grants, converts major income support programs into state-administered block grants, and wipes out the federal guarantee of funds for all those who apply for aid. Without the federal back-up, fiscally strapped states will not be able to serve all those in need when the population grows or the economy sinks. You'd never guess from all the fuss that the $24 billion spent on AFDC benefits in 1994 represented only 1 percent of the federal budget—4 percent when Medicaid and food stamps are included.

Despite all this, I can end on an optimistic note. Poor and middle class women are not taking the blame, the punishment, or the coercion lying down. Since 1987, poor women have been fighting the war on the poor through such groups as the National Welfare Rights Union. This time around, they have been joined by large numbers of welfare advocates who are also working to limit punitive policies and to secure "real" welfare reform. Reversing past practice, these activists are spanning the traditional schisms between welfare recipients, feminist activists, and human service workers. The infrastructure built up during the past ten years [since 1985] of fighting right-wing social policies was mobilized on Valentine's Day, 1995, when organizations in 38 states and 77 cities from Maine to Hawaii participated in a national day of action to stop the war on the poor. This growing network is now well-positioned to be mobilized again, and again, and again.

These grassroots actions are critical. The historical record shows that the powers that be rarely act and social change rarely occurs for the better unless pressured from below. Unless today's politicians know that we mean business, they will not budge.

4

Welfare Reform Must Protect Children and Legal Immigrants

Bill Clinton

Bill Clinton took office as the forty-second U.S. president in January 1993.

The bipartisan welfare reform act of 1996 will finally put an end to America's failed welfare system by stressing work and responsibility. This legislation enhances the enforcement of child-support laws, provides billions of dollars for child care to help mothers on welfare become working mothers, protects nutritional assistance to children in welfare families, and guarantees health care to Americans on welfare. However, Congress should correct some flawed provisions of the act, such as the reduction of nutritional assistance to children of working families and the denial of welfare benefits to legal immigrants.

Editor's Note: The following statement was given on July 31, 1996, the same day that the U.S. Senate passed the Personal Responsibility and Work Opportunity Reconciliation Act of 1996.

When I ran for President in 1992, I pledged to end welfare as we know it. I have worked very hard for four years to do just that.

Today the Congress will vote on legislation that gives us a chance to live up to that promise, to transform a broken system that traps too many people in a cycle of dependence to one that emphasizes work and independence, to give people on welfare a chance to draw a paycheck, not a welfare check. It gives us a better chance to give those on welfare what we want for all families in America, the opportunity to succeed at home and at work.

For those reasons, I will sign it into law.

The legislation is, however, far from perfect. There are parts of it that are wrong, and I will work—I will address those parts in a moment. But

From Bill Clinton's remarks at a news conference, July 31, 1996, courtesy of the Federal News Service.

on balance, this bill is a real step forward for our country, our values, and for people who are on welfare.

For 15 years I have worked on this problem, as Governor and as the President. I've spent time in welfare offices, I have talked to mothers on welfare who desperately want the chance to work and support their families independently.

A long time ago I concluded that the current welfare system undermines the basic values of work, responsibility and family, trapping generation after generation in dependency and hurting the very people it was designed to help.

Today we have an historic opportunity to make welfare what it was meant to be: a second chance, not a way of life. And even though the bill has serious flaws that are unrelated to welfare reform, I believe we have a duty to seize the opportunity it gives us to end welfare as we know it.

[Welfare reform] should give people the child care and the health care they need to move from welfare to work without hurting their children.

Since 1993, I have done everything in my power as President to promote work and responsibility, working with 41 states to give them 69 welfare-reform experiments. We've also required teen mothers to stay in school, required Federal employees to pay their child support, cracked down on people who owe child support and cross state lines. As a result, child-support collections are up 40 percent to $11 billion, and there are 1.3 million fewer people on welfare today than there were when I took office.

From the outset, however, I have also worked with members of both parties in Congress to achieve a national welfare reform bill that will make work and responsibility the law of the land.

What welfare reform should do

I made my principles for real welfare reform very clear from the beginning. First and foremost, it should be about moving people from welfare to work. It should impose time limits on welfare. It should give people the child care and the health care they need to move from welfare to work without hurting their children. It should crack down on child-support enforcement, and it should protect our children.

This legislation meets these principles. It gives us a chance we haven't had before to break the cycle of dependency that has existed for millions and millions of our fellow citizens, exiling them from the world of work. It gives structure, meaning and dignity to most of our lives.

We've come a long way in this debate. It's important to remember that not so very long ago, at the beginning of this 104th Congress, some wanted to put poor children in orphanages and take away all help from mothers simply because they were poor, young and unmarried. In 1995 the Republican majority in Congress sent me legislation [Personal Responsibility and Work Opportunity Act of 1995] that had its priorities backward: It was soft on work and tough on children. It failed to provide child care and health care. It imposed deep and unacceptable cuts in school lunches, child welfare and help for disabled children.

The bill came to me twice, and I vetoed it twice. The bipartisan legislation before the Congress today is significantly better than the bills I vetoed. Many of the worst elements I objected to are out of it, and many of the improvements I asked for are included.

What the bill achieves

First, the new bill is strong on work. It provides $4 billion more for child care so that mothers can move from welfare to work, and protects their children by maintaining health and safety standards for day care.

These things are very important. You cannot ask somebody on welfare to go to work if they're going to neglect their children in doing it.

It gives states powerful performance incentives to place people in jobs. It requires states to hold up their end of the bargain by maintaining their own spending on welfare. And it gives states the capacity to create jobs by taking money now used for welfare checks and giving it to employers as income subsidies, as an incentive to hire people, or being used to create community service jobs.

Second, this new bill is better for children than the two I vetoed. It keeps the national nutritional safety net intact by eliminating the food stamp cap and the optional block grant. It drops the deep cuts and devastating changes in school lunch, child welfare and help for disabled children. It allows states to use Federal money to provide vouchers to children whose parents can't find work after the time limits expire. And it preserves the national guarantee of health care for poor children, the disabled, pregnant women, the elderly and people on welfare.

Just as important, this bill continues to include the child-support enforcement measures I proposed in 1994, the most sweeping crackdown on deadbeat parents in history.

If every parent paid the child support they should, we could move 800,000 women and children off welfare immediately. With this bill, we say to parents, if you don't pay the child support you owe, we will garnish your wages, take away your driver's license, track you across state lines and, if necessary, make you work off what you owe.

It is a very important advance that could only be achieved in legislation. I did not have the executive authority to do this without a bill.

I am deeply disappointed that the Congressional leadership insisted on attaching . . . a provision that will hurt legal immigrants.

So I will sign this bill, first and foremost, because the current system is broken; second, because Congress has made many of the changes I sought; and third, because even though serious problems remain in the non-welfare-reform provisions of the bill, this is the best chance we will have for a long, long time to complete the work of ending welfare as we know it, by moving people from welfare to work, demanding responsibility, and doing better by children.

Two areas of concern

However, I want to be very clear. Some parts of this bill still go too far, and I am determined to see that those areas are corrected.

First, I am concerned that although we have made great strides to maintain the national nutritional safety net, this bill still cuts deeper than it should in nutritional assistance, mostly for working families with children.

In the budget talks, we reached a tentative agreement on $21 billion in food stamp savings over the next several years. They are included in this bill. However, the Congressional majority insisted on another cut we did not agree to, repealing a reform adopted in 1992 in Congress, which was to go into effect in 1997. It's called the excess shelter reduction, which helped some of our hardest-pressed working families [by giving those with excessive housing costs increased food stamp benefits]. Finally, we were going to treat working families with children the same way we treat senior citizens who draw food stamps today.

Now, blocking this change I believe—I know—will make it harder for some of our hardest-pressed working families with children. This provision is a mistake, and I will work to correct it.

Second, I am deeply disappointed that the Congressional leadership insisted on attaching to this extraordinarily important bill a provision that will hurt legal immigrants in America, people who work hard for their families, pay taxes, serve in our military. This provision has nothing to do with welfare reform; it is simply a budget-saving measure, and it is not right.

All of us have to . . . see this reform not as a chance to demonize or demean anyone.

These immigrant families with children, who fall on hard times through no fault of their own—for example, because they face the same risks the rest of us do from accidents, from criminal assaults, from serious illness—they should be eligible for medical and other help when they need it.

The Republican majority could never have passed such a provision standing alone. You see that in the debate in the 1996 immigration bill—for example, over the Gallegly amendment [which would allow states to bar children of undocumented immigrants from public education]—and the question of education of undocumented and illegal immigrant children.

This provision will cause great stress for states, for localities, for medical facilities that have to serve a large number of legal immigrants. It is just wrong to say to people, "We'll let you work here; you're helping our country. You'll pay taxes. You serve in our military. You may get killed defending America. But if somebody mugs you on a street corner, or you get cancer, or you get hit by a car, or the same thing happens to your children, we're not going to give you assistance anymore."

I am convinced this would never have passed alone, and I am convinced when we send legislation to Congress to correct it, it will be corrected.

In the meantime, let me also say that I intend to take further executive action directing the INS [Immigration and Naturalization Service] to continue to work to remove the bureaucratic roadblocks to citizenship to all eligible legal immigrants. I will do everything in my power, in other words, to make sure that this bill lifts people up and does not become an excuse for anyone to turn their backs on this problem or on people who are genuinely in need, through no fault of their own.

What states and businesses must do

This bill must also not let anyone off the hook. The states asked for this responsibility; now they have to shoulder it and not run away from it. We have to make sure that in the coming years, reform and change actually result in moving people from welfare to work. The business community must provide greater private-sector jobs that people on welfare need to build good lives and strong families.

I challenge every state to adopt the reforms that Wisconsin, Oregon, Missouri and other states are proposing to do, to take the money that used to be available for welfare checks and offer it to the private sector as wage subsidies to begin to hire these people, to give them a chance to build their families and build their lives.

All of us have to rise to this challenge and see this reform not as a chance to demonize or demean anyone, but instead as an opportunity to bring everyone fully into the mainstream of American life, to give them a chance to share in the prosperity and the promise that most of our people are enjoying today. And we here in Washington must continue to do everything in our power to reward work and to expand opportunity for all people.

The earned-income tax credit [EITC], which we expanded in 1993 dramatically, is now rewarding the work of 15 million working families. I am pleased that Congressional efforts to gut this tax cut for the hardest-pressed working people have been blocked. This legislation preserves the EITC and its benefits for working families.

Now we must increase the minimum wage, which also will benefit millions of working people with families and help them to offset the impact of some of the nutritional cuts in this bill.

Through these efforts we all have to recognize, as I said in 1992, the best antipoverty program is still a job.

I want to congratulate the members of Congress in both parties who worked together on this welfare reform legislation. I want to challenge them to put politics aside and continue to work together to meet our other challenges, and to correct the problems that are still there with this legislation.

I am convinced that it does present an historic opportunity to finish the work of ending welfare as we know it, and that is why I have decided to sign it.

5

Welfare Reform Is Necessary

Robert Rector

Robert Rector is a senior policy analyst and welfare researcher at the Heritage Foundation, a Washington, D.C., think tank that promotes conservatism and free enterprise.

Since the beginning of the War on Poverty in 1965, government spending on welfare has skyrocketed, with per-person spending increasing fivefold. This prolific spending has contributed to a breakdown in values and conduct among the poor. The welfare system discourages two-parent families from remaining intact and has destroyed the family structure in low-income communities. Welfare reform must achieve reductions in illegitimacy, increase the stability of two-parent families, bring soaring welfare costs under control, and establish serious work requirements for able-bodied welfare recipients.

Since World War II, Presidents and Members of Congress have promised American taxpayers that they would reform, in a serious way, America's failed welfare system. The reality, however, is that the system keeps growing, new programs are introduced when earlier reforms do not work, and the level of spending on federal and state welfare programs continues to increase.

There is a growing consensus that the current welfare system is a disaster, not only for taxpayers who are required to pay ever larger amounts of money to maintain and expand the system, but also for the poor who supposedly are being helped by it. While liberals and conservatives agree that the current welfare system is badly broken, only conservatives have been prepared to take the steps to achieve structural reform—in 1995, liberals actually fought to block reform. In the election of 1996, conservative candidates need to articulate the clear choice. In particular, they must remind voters that:

President Bill Clinton promised serious welfare reform, but when Congress sent him legislation [in December 1995 and January 1996] that would have accomplished this, he vetoed it. Welfare reform remains a major domestic issue for the President and Congress. While the President promised in 1992 "to end welfare as we know it," the Clinton Administration's bill

Robert Rector, "Welfare Reform," in *Issues '96: The Candidate's Briefing Book*; © 1996 by The Heritage Foundation. Reprinted with permission [the Work and Personal Responsibility Act of 1994] did nothing of the sort. It did not stop exploding welfare costs. It did not establish meaningful work requirements. And it did not address the persistent problem of additional out-of-wedlock births among women who are getting welfare benefits. While the President's bill proposed a two-year time limit on welfare, a reading of the fine print revealed that it merely placed a few welfare recipients in government "make work" jobs while allowing them to remain on welfare. Moreover, the work requirements were truly weak. The bill required only 7 percent of the welfare population to enroll in the work program by 1999, and would have required those enrolled to work for only 15 hours per week. Worse, instead of controlling spending, the Clinton plan would have continued the automatic and rapid growth of welfare spending.

First, and most important, welfare reform must seek to reduce the illegitimate birth rate and promote the formation of stable two-parent families.

On the other hand, Congress passed a serious welfare reform bill that establishes serious work requirements, addresses the problem of illegitimacy, and slows the growth in federal welfare spending. The President vetoed this bill.

Current welfare costs are rising, and without some fiscal discipline imposed by Congress, taxpayers will be saddled with enormous future tax burdens. There are 77 overlapping welfare programs to assist Americans officially designated as poor. Total welfare spending in the United States exceeds $324 billion, or over $3,400 for each taxpaying household in the United States. Of this spending, 72 percent is federal and 28 percent is state. About 90 percent of all state welfare spending is on federally designed welfare programs.

Liberals in Congress strongly support federal welfare programs, defend the current rate of spending for these programs, and oppose even modest reductions in the rate of growth of welfare spending. At current rates, the United States will be spending $500 billion on welfare by 1999, or a full 6 percent of the gross national product (GNP). Under current federal spending scenarios, this would mean $2 on welfare for every $1 we now spend on national defense.

Most important, serious welfare reform must address the illegitimacy crisis. In 1959, 28 percent of poor families with children were headed by women. By 1991, 61 percent of poor families with children were headed by single women. The illegitimate birth rate among white high school dropouts is now a stunning 48 percent.

Aside from its relationship to federal welfare policy, America's overall rate of illegitimacy is a social catastrophe. The social science literature on the subject is unambiguous and indisputable: Children born out of wedlock do not have the same chances in life as do children born into intact two-parent families. Children born out of wedlock have lower levels of educational achievement, lower economic achievement, increased psychological and behavioral problems, and a greater propensity to substance abuse, juvenile delinquency, and crime. For the President and Congress, the key relationship between the growing problem of illegitimacy and welfare policy is this: Should illegitimacy be the basis of a government entitlement to benefits? Americans either are or are not going to subsidize illegitimacy. There are no compromises on this point.

Needed: a serious policy for welfare reform

In overhauling this failed system, policymakers should be guided by the following four themes:

1. *Reduce illegitimacy.* First, and most important, welfare reform must seek to reduce the illegitimate birth rate and promote the formation of stable two-parent families. Any "reform" that does not dramatically reduce the illegitimate birth rate will not save money and will fail to help America's children.

2. *Demand reciprocity and work.* Reform must convert welfare from a one-way handout into a system of mutual responsibility in which welfare recipients are given aid but also are expected to contribute something to society for the assistance given.

3. *Get costs under control.* Reform must control soaring welfare costs, which are slowly bankrupting the nation.

4. *Promote moral renewal.* Halting the growth of the underclass ultimately will require not only welfare reform, but also moral and cultural renewal. The government can assist in the process of moral rebuilding by allowing private social institutions, such as churches and other community institutions, to play a far greater role in educating and shaping the moral code of young people. Among other steps needed to do this, parents must be given far greater choice in how their children are educated, including the right to use government vouchers to send their children to religious schools.

The cost of the welfare system amounted to $3,357 in taxes from each household that paid federal income tax in 1993.

Social collapse over the last 30 years has coincided with growth in the welfare state. The U.S. welfare system may be defined as the total set of government programs, federal and state, explicitly designed to assist poor and low-income Americans. Current welfare assistance has three ostensible objectives:

1. *Sustaining* living standards through cash and non-cash transfers,
2. *Promoting* self-sufficiency, and
3. *Aiding* economically distressed communities.

Most welfare programs are individually means-tested. Means-tested programs restrict eligibility for benefits to persons with non-welfare income below a certain level. Individuals with non-welfare income above a specified cutoff level cannot receive aid. Thus, for example, food stamps and Aid to Families with Dependent Children (AFDC) are means-tested, and thus constitute welfare, but Social Security benefits are not. Some 94 percent of total welfare spending takes the form of means-tested aid given directly to individuals.

Other welfare programs are community-targeted or categorical. Community-targeted programs provide assistance to communities which contain a high percentage of poor and low-income persons or are economically distressed. Some 5.2 percent of welfare spending is directed through programs of this kind. Pure categorical programs provide aid to specific disadvantaged or generally needy groups, such as migrant farmworkers, homeless persons, or abandoned children, without a formal means test. Only 1.2 percent of total welfare spending is dedicated to simple categorical programs.

In constant dollars, federal, state, and local welfare spending rose from $158 billion in 1975 to $324 billion in 1993.

The federal government currently runs 77 major interrelated and overlapping welfare programs. Many states also operate their own independent programs. This federal and state welfare system now includes cash aid, food, medical aid, housing aid, energy aid, jobs and training, targeted and means-tested education, social service, and urban and community development programs. A list of the 80 major federal and state welfare programs covered in this viewpoint is provided in the Heritage Foundation monograph *America's Failed $5.4 Trillion War on Poverty.*[1]

• In 1993, 48 percent of total welfare spending was devoted to medical programs. Cash programs took 22.1 percent. Food, housing, and energy programs comprised 18.8 percent of the total, while education aid, job training, social services, and urban and community aid accounted for 11.1 percent.

• Total federal and state spending on welfare programs was $324.3 billion in FY [fiscal year] 1993. Of that total, $234.3 billion (72 percent) came from federal funding and $90 billion (28 percent) came from state or local funds.

• Welfare spending is so large it is difficult to comprehend. One way to make it more tangible is to recognize that, on average, the cost of the welfare system amounted to $3,357 in taxes from each household that paid federal income tax in 1993.

• Federal and state welfare spending is now the third largest category of total government spending, ranking below the first (combined Social Security and Medicare) and second (total government spending on general education) but above the fourth (national defense).

How the welfare state has grown[2]

For the first 150 years of U.S. history, the government played little role in welfare.[3] Charity or welfare was conducted largely by private religious organizations.

As late as 1929, before the onset of the Great Depression, federal, state, and local welfare expenditures were only $90 million. Adjusted into

1993 dollars, this would be $813 million. Public-sector welfare spending in 1929 amounted to $6.68 per person in 1993 dollars. (Unless noted otherwise, all spending figures in this section have been adjusted for inflation into constant 1993 dollars.)

Charts 1 and 2 show the growth in welfare since 1929. The Great Depression, which threw nearly a quarter of the labor force out of work, led to a dramatic change in government welfare spending. Expenditures for work relief welfare programs such as the Civilian Conservation Corps, Works Progress Administration, and Civil Works Administration grew rapidly. By 1939, welfare spending hit a peak of $46.6 billion—compared with less than $1 billion in 1929 (expressed in 1993 dollars).

Chart 1. History of Total Welfare Spending

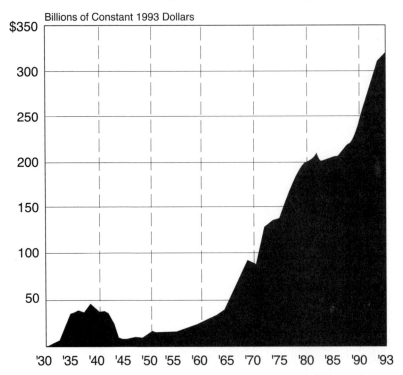

Source: Robert Rector and William F. Lauber, America's Failed $5.4 Trillion War on Poverty, 1995.

In inflation-adjusted terms, welfare spending would not return to the 1939 peak until the onset of the War on Poverty a quarter-century later. The major Great Depression anti-poverty programs were terminated at the beginning of World War II. In the post-war period, welfare spending remained low relative to the 1930s.

Chart 2. Welfare Spending by Program Type: Federal, State, and Local

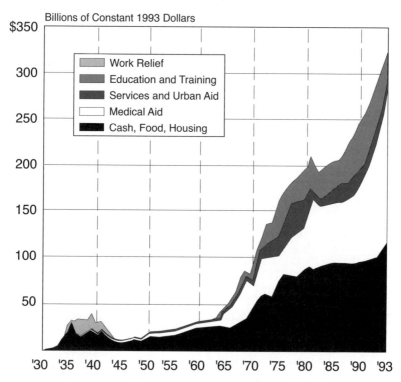

Billions of Constant 1993 Dollars

Legend:
- Work Relief
- Education and Training
- Services and Urban Aid
- Medical Aid
- Cash, Food, Housing

Source: Robert Rector and William F. Lauber, America's Failed $5.4 Trillion War on Poverty, 1995.

In 1950, total welfare spending by federal, state, and local governments was $18.8 billion (in 1993 dollars), less than the cost of the food stamp program alone in 1993. During the 1950s and early 1960s, welfare spending grew slowly, reaching $34.9 billion in 1964 at the onset of the War on Poverty. In 1964, welfare absorbed 1.2 percent of gross domestic product (GDP) as compared with 1.1 percent in 1950.

In his 1964 State of the Union address, President Lyndon Johnson announced the "War on Poverty." New legislation and spending initiatives began to take effect by 1965. Between 1965 and 1970, over two dozen separate federal welfare programs were created. Eligibility for older programs, such as Aid to Families with Dependent Children and food stamps, was expanded. In three years (1965–1968), welfare spending in constant dollars more than doubled, rising from $38.3 billion to $80.5 billion.

In the first decade of the War on Poverty, there was explosive growth in all categories of welfare spending.

Between 1965 and 1975, measured in constant dollars, cash aid nearly tripled, social service spending tripled, medical aid almost quintupled, food aid did quintuple, housing spending increased sevenfold, and job training funds increased fifteenfold. By 1975, total welfare spending had reached $119.4 billion (in constant 1993 dollars), almost a fivefold increase compared with 1965 levels after adjusting for inflation. While total welfare spending absorbed 1.3 percent of GDP in 1965, just ten years later, some 3.8 percent of the economy was devoted to welfare.

Since 1975 welfare spending has continued to grow rapidly, although not at the record pace of the 1965–1975 decade. In constant dollars, federal, state, and local welfare spending rose from $158 billion in 1975 to $324 billion in 1993. After adjusting for inflation, welfare spending has risen in every year but two from 1965 to the present. Welfare spending is now 8.4 times greater than in 1965 when the War on Poverty began. Cash, food, housing, and energy aid are six times greater today than when the War on Poverty began.

Charts 1 and 2 also belie the political myth that President Reagan slashed welfare spending. As the charts clearly show, welfare spending grew during Reagan's presidency. Total welfare spending was $199 billion in 1980 when Ronald Reagan was elected President. By 1988, his last year in office, welfare spending reached $230 billion. Cash, food, housing, and energy spending rose from $89 billion to $102 billion over the same period (all figures in constant 1993 dollars). Ronald Reagan did not reduce welfare spending; he merely slowed its explosive growth rate.

Claims that Reagan cut welfare spending utilize the simple trick of selecting one or two programs in the list of 80 welfare programs and deliberately not counting the rest. By selecting one or two programs that have been reduced while ignoring the rapid growth in the other 78, it is possible to "prove" in every single year that welfare has been "slashed" when in fact aggregate spending continues to increase.

While Reagan slowed the growth of welfare spending, it exploded during the George Bush presidency at rates that rivaled those of the late 1960s. In constant 1993 dollars, total welfare spending rose from $224 billion in 1988, when Bush was elected, to $324 billion in 1993, when Clinton assumed the presidency: a $100 billion increase in five years.

Spending per low-income person

A second way of examining the growth of welfare spending is to compare spending increases with the growth of the U.S. population. Chart 3 shows total welfare spending divided by the number of persons in the lowest income quarter of the population. This calculation provides a reasonably accurate picture of the level of welfare resources available relative to the pool of potential recipients.[4] Chart 3 reveals a now-familiar pattern.

Welfare spending per low-income person was nearly zero in 1929 but shot up during the Great Depression, reaching a peak of $1,419 per low-income person (in 1993 dollars). After World War II, spending fell to low levels and remained relatively constant until the start of the War on Poverty in 1965. Between 1965 and 1975, spending exploded, growing from $789 per person to $2,938 (both figures in 1993 dollars). Spending grew moderately during the Jimmy Carter years, leveling off during the Reagan presidency and then exploding again during the Bush era.

By 1993, total welfare spending per low-income person reached $5,023. In constant dollars, this was three times higher than the peak level in the Great Depression.

Chart 4 shows the same trends in per capita spending but limits welfare spending figures to cash, food, housing, and energy aid. As in the previous chart, welfare spending (in this case cash, food, housing, and energy) is divided by the number of persons in the lowest income quarter of the population. The chart clearly rebuts the claim that the growth in welfare spending has been limited to medical programs. The pattern is identical to that of the previous charts.

In constant dollars, welfare spending for the limited basic programs peaked during the Great Depression, remained relatively low and constant during the 1950s and 1960s, exploded upward at the onset of the War on Poverty, and remained in a nearly vertical climb until the mid-1970s. Spending leveled off during the Reagan years and spiked sharply upward again in the late 1980s and early 1990s.

In constant dollars, cash, food, housing, and energy aid per person is nearly five times higher today than at the beginning of the War on Poverty.

With the onset of the War on Poverty, a massive share of the economy was rapidly diverted to welfare programs.

Another way to assess the growth in welfare spending is to measure the share of the total economy which is absorbed by welfare. Chart 5 shows total federal, state, and local welfare spending as a percentage of gross domestic product. The data match the patterns shown in Charts 1 through 4.

During the Great Depression, welfare spending rose to around 4 percent of GDP, peaking at 4.8 percent in 1939. The growth of spending as a share of GDP was driven both by increases in real spending and by shrinkage in the size of the economy due to the Depression. It is also important to note that most welfare spending during the Depression was for work relief programs, such as the Civilian Conservation Corps, which bear little resemblance to most of today's welfare programs.

After World War II, welfare spending fell to 0.5 percent of GDP. It rose to slightly over 1 percent in 1950 and remained at that level through the early 1960s.

With the onset of the War on Poverty, a massive share of the economy was rapidly diverted to welfare programs. Welfare spending rose to over 4 percent by the mid-1970s. During the Reagan years, a slowdown in the growth of spending, coupled with a growing economy, led to slight declines in welfare as a share of GDP. By 1988, welfare spending was 3.75 percent of GDP. The Bush era quickly reversed this trend; by 1993, welfare constituted 5.08 percent of GDP, a new record level exceeding the previous peak set during the Great Depression.

Chart 3. Welfare Spending per Low-Income Person

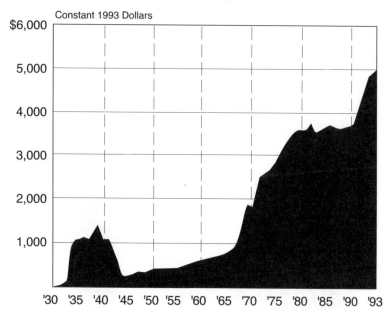

Chart 4. Welfare Cash, Food, Housing, and Energy Aid per Low-Income Person

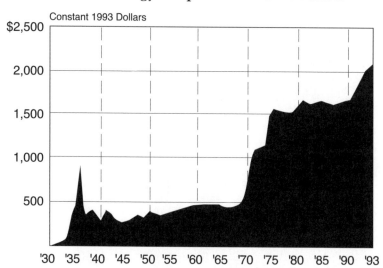

Note: Figures equal spending divided by lowest income quarter of population.
Source: Robert Rector and William F. Lauber, America's Failed $5.4 Trillion War on Poverty, 1995.

Chart 5. Total Welfare Spending as a Share of Gross Domestic Product: Federal, State, and Local

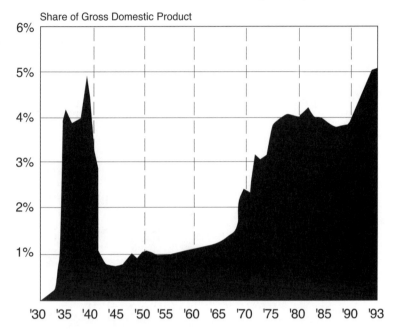

Source: Robert Rector and William F. Lauber, America's Failed $5.4 Trillion War on Poverty, 1995.

A final way to assess the growth in welfare spending is to compare it to the increase in spending on other government functions (Chart 6).

• Since the onset of the War on Poverty, means-tested welfare spending by federal, state, and local governments has grown more rapidly than spending on all other major government functions.

• In 1965, the U.S. spent 17 cents on welfare for each dollar spent on national defense. By 1993, this had risen to $1.11 on welfare for each dollar spent on defense.

• In 1965, the U.S. spent 29 cents on welfare for every dollar spent on primary, secondary, and post-secondary education by all levels of government. By 1993, the U.S. spent 91 cents on welfare for every dollar spent on education.[5]

• In 1965, the U.S. spent 51 cents on welfare for each dollar spent on Social Security and Medicare. By 1993, 77 cents was spent on welfare for each dollar spent on Social Security and Medicare.[6]

Even if the analysis is restricted to welfare spending on cash, food, housing, and energy programs, the trends are virtually identical. Since the beginning of the War on Poverty, means-tested cash, food, housing, and energy programs have grown more rapidly than defense, education, or Social Security.

• In 1965, the U.S. spent 16 cents on cash, food, housing, and energy welfare aid for each dollar spent on Social Security. By 1993, the figure had risen to 43 cents.

Total cost of the War on Poverty

The financial cost of the War on Poverty has been enormous.

Between 1965 and 1994, welfare spending cost taxpayers $5.4 trillion in constant 1993 dollars.

As Chart 7 shows, out of total welfare spending of $5.4 trillion, cash welfare programs cost $1.3 trillion. Medical programs assisting low-income persons cost $2.1 trillion. Spending on food programs equaled $599 billion, while housing and energy aid programs for low-income persons cost $489 billion. Special education programs for low-income children cost $319 billion, and jobs and training programs cost $215 billion. An additional $227 billion was spent on special social services for the poor, and $171 billion was spent on development aid for low-income communities.

The figure $5.4 trillion is difficult to comprehend. Chart 8 offers some comparisons. As the chart indicates, the cost of fighting World War II was $3.1 trillion (expressed in 1993 dollars). The cost of the War on Poverty has been some 70 percent greater than the price tag for defeating Germany and Japan in World War II, after adjusting for inflation.[7]

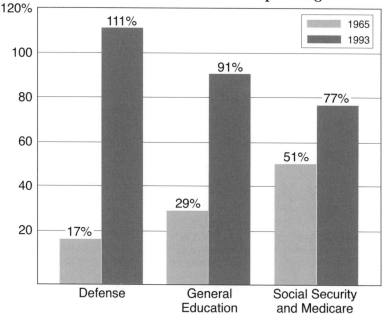

Chart 6. Welfare Spending as a Percentage of Other Government Spending

Source: Robert Rector and William F. Lauber, America's Failed $5.4 Trillion War on Poverty, 1995.

Chart 7. Total Spending on the
War on Poverty: 1965–1994

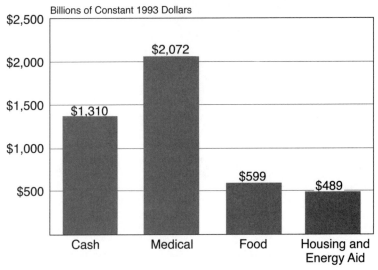

Billions of Constant 1993 Dollars

- $2,500
- $2,000
- $1,500
- $1,000
- $500

$2,072
$1,310
$599
$489

Cash   Medical   Food   Housing and Energy Aid

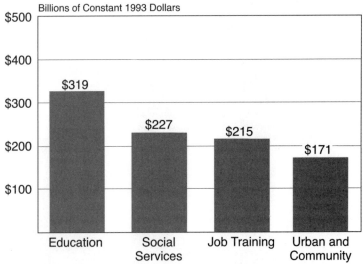

Billions of Constant 1993 Dollars

- $500
- $400
- $300
- $200
- $100

$319
$227
$215
$171

Education   Social Services   Job Training   Urban and Community

Note: Includes federal, state, and local spending. Fiscal year 1994 spending was estimated at 1993 levels.
Source: Robert Rector and William F. Lauber, America's Failed $5.4 Trillion War on Poverty, 1995.

As Chart 8 also shows, the $5.4 trillion cost of the War on Poverty nearly equals the entire cost of the private-sector industrial and business infrastructure of the U.S.[8] For $5.4 trillion one can purchase every factory, all the manufacturing equipment, and every office building in the U.S. With the leftover funds, one could go on to purchase every airline, every railroad, every trucking firm, the entire commercial maritime fleet, every telephone, television, and radio company, every power company, every hotel, and every retail and wholesale store in the nation.[9]

It is interesting to note the total cost of the many peripheral programs which often are ignored in calculating the cost of welfare or the War on Poverty. For example, the $172 billion spent on urban and community development is nearly enough to buy the entire plant and equipment of every auto manufacturer, every airline, and every trucking company in the U.S. The $445 billion price tag for job training and social services for low-income Americans would purchase all the steel plants, all the factories producing new industrial equipment, all the electronics manufacturing plants, and all the furniture plants in the U.S., as well as the whole U.S. commercial maritime fleet. With the $440 billion which the government has spent in housing and energy aid, one could purchase the entire U.S. construction industry, all the hotels in the U.S., and the entire chemical industry.

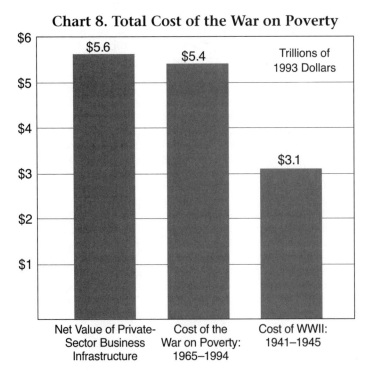

Chart 8. Total Cost of the War on Poverty

Net Value of Private-Sector Business Infrastructure: $5.6 (Trillions of 1993 Dollars)
Cost of the War on Poverty: 1965–1994: $5.4
Cost of WWII: 1941–1945: $3.1

Source: Robert Rector and William F. Lauber, America's Failed $5.4 Trillion War on Poverty, 1995.

Two kinds of poverty

The growth of the welfare state has had a huge impact on U.S. society. In order to unravel its effects, policymakers must begin by understanding two separate concepts: "material poverty" and "behavioral poverty."

Material poverty. Material poverty means, in the simplest sense, having a family income below the official poverty income threshold, which was $14,763 for a family of four in 1993. To the man on the street, to say someone is poor implies that he is malnourished, poorly clothed, and living in filthy, dilapidated, and overcrowded housing. In reality, there is little material poverty in the U.S. as the public generally understands the term.[10]

The $5.4 trillion cost of the War on Poverty nearly equals the entire cost of the private-sector industrial and business infrastructure of the U.S.

In 1990, after adjusting for inflation, per capita expenditures of the lowest income one-fifth of the U.S. population exceeded the per capita income of the median American household in 1960.[11] There is little or no poverty-induced malnutrition in the U.S. Persons defined as poor by the U.S. government have almost the same average consumption of protein, vitamins, and other nutrients as persons in the upper middle class.[12]

Children living in poverty today, far from being malnourished, actually grow up to be one inch taller and ten pounds heavier than the average child of the same age in the general population in the late 1950s.[13] The principal nutrition-related problem facing poor persons in the U.S. today is obesity, not hunger; the poor have a higher rate of obesity than do members of other socioeconomic groups in the U.S.

Similarly, poor Americans have more housing space and are less likely to be overcrowded than is the average citizen in Western Europe.[14] Nearly all of America's poor live in decent housing that is reasonably well-maintained. In fact, nearly 40 percent of the households defined as poor by the U.S. government actually own their own homes.[15]

Behavioral poverty. Behavioral poverty, by contrast, refers to a breakdown in the values and conduct which lead to the formation of healthy families, stable personalities, and self-sufficiency. Behavioral poverty incorporates a cluster of severe social pathologies, including eroded work ethic and dependency, lack of educational aspiration and achievement, inability or unwillingness to control one's children, increased single parenthood and illegitimacy, criminal activity, and drug and alcohol abuse. While material poverty may be rare in the United States, behavioral poverty is abundant and growing at an alarming pace.

The core dilemma of the welfare state is that prolific spending intended to alleviate material poverty has led to a dramatic increase in behavioral poverty. In welfare, as in other government policies, you get what you pay for. The current welfare system heavily subsidizes illegitimacy, divorce, and non-work. The past 25 years have seen dramatic increases in all three behaviors. The War on Poverty may have raised the material standard of living of a few Americans, but it has done so at the cost of creating whole communities where traditional two-parent families have vanished, work is rare or nonexistent, and multiple generations have grown up dependent on government transfers. The disintegration of the family encouraged by the current welfare system has led in turn to other severe social problems, particularly a dramatic increase in crime.

The anti-marriage and anti-work effects of welfare are simple and profound. The current welfare system may be conceptualized best as a system that offers each single mother with two children a "paycheck" of combined benefits worth an average of between $8,500 and $15,000, depending on the state.[16] The mother has a contract with the government. She will continue to receive her "paycheck" as long as she fulfills two conditions:

Condition #1: She must not work.
Condition #2: She must not marry an employed male.[17]

Thus, the current welfare system provides heavy incentives for individuals to work less or leave the labor force entirely and rely on the taxpayers for support. Even worse, welfare has made marriage economically irrational for most low-income parents; it has converted the low-income working husband from a necessary breadwinner into a net financial handicap.[18] It has transformed marriage from a legal institution designed to protect and nurture children into an institution that financially penalizes nearly all low-income parents who enter into it.

Welfare also engenders long-term inter-generational dependence. Of the over 4.5 million families currently receiving assistance through Aid to Families with Dependent Children (AFDC), well over half will remain dependent for over ten years, many for 15 years or longer.[19] Moreover, dependence passes between generations; children raised in families that receive welfare assistance are three times more likely to be on welfare than other children when they become adults.[20]

This inter-generational dependency is a clear indication that the welfare system is failing in its goal to lift the poor from poverty to self-sufficiency and is trapping many families in a repeating cycle of debilitating and self-destructive behavior.

Effects of welfare

The growth of the welfare state has coincided with a decline in labor force attachment. In 1960, among the lowest income quintile of the population, nearly two-thirds of households were headed by persons who worked.[21] By 1991, this figure had fallen to around one-third, and only 11 percent were headed by persons who worked full-time throughout the year.[22]

Part of this decline in employment can be attributed to the increasing number of retired elderly households in this income group, but an equally important factor is the decline in labor force participation among non-elderly heads of households.

For a growing number of poor Americans, the existence of generous welfare programs makes not working a reasonable alternative to long-term employment. During the late 1960s and early 1970s, social scientists at the Office of Economic Opportunity (OEO) conducted a series of controlled experiments to examine the effect of welfare benefits on work effort. The longest running and most comprehensive of these experiments was conducted between 1971 and 1978 in Seattle and Denver and became known as the Seattle/Denver Income Maintenance Experiment, or "SIME/DIME."[23]

Advocates of expanding welfare had hoped that SIME/DIME and similar experiments conducted in other cities would prove that generous welfare benefits did not adversely affect work effort. Instead, the SIME/DIME experiment found that each $1.00 of extra welfare given to low-income persons reduced labor and earnings by an average of $0.80.[24] The significant anti-work effects of welfare benefits were shown in all social groups, including married women, single mothers, and husbands. They were particularly pronounced among young unmarried males; the number of hours worked per week declined 43 percent for those who remained unmarried throughout the experiment and 33 percent for those who married.[25] The results of the SIME/DIME study apply directly to existing welfare programs: Nearly all have strong anti-work effects like those studied in this experiment.

Research by Dr. June O'Neill of New York's Baruch College, now Director of the Congressional Budget Office, confirms that higher welfare benefits increase the number of individuals who leave the labor force and enroll in welfare. A 50 percent increase in monthly AFDC and food stamp benefit levels was found to lead to a 75 percent increase both in the number of women enrolling in AFDC and in the number of years spent on AFDC.[26] In other words, increases in benefit value cause a dramatic expansion in welfare caseloads.

An extremely important research discovery by O'Neill is that high AFDC benefits reduce the employment of young adult men even though few, if any, of these men benefit directly from AFDC payments. High AFDC benefits were found to reduce the employment of young adult men in a community by some 50 percent. High benefit levels apparently affect the work behavior of young men in two ways. First, they reduce the probability of marriage and thereby reduce the necessity for a young man to work to support a family. Second, it is likely that many young single men who are boyfriends to single mothers on AFDC indirectly share in the mothers' welfare benefits; higher benefits thereby reduce their need for work.[27]

The welfare system is . . . trapping many families in a repeating cycle of debilitating and self-destructive behavior.

The onset of the War on Poverty coincided with the disintegration of the low-income family—the black family in particular. At the outset of World War II, the black illegitimate birth rate was slightly less than 19 percent. Between 1955 and 1965, it rose slowly from 22 percent in 1955 to 28 percent in 1965. Beginning in the late 1960s, however, the rate of black illegitimate births skyrocketed—reaching 49 percent in 1975 and 69 percent in 1993.

If current trends continue, the black illegitimate birth rate will reach 75 percent within ten years.[28] Rapid increases in illegitimacy also are occurring among low-income whites; the illegitimate birth rate among white high school dropouts is 48 percent. Overall, 30 percent of American children are born to single mothers.

The welfare system has all but destroyed family structure in low-income communities.

Across the nation, the welfare system has all but destroyed family structure in low-income communities. Welfare establishes strong financial disincentives which effectively block the formation of intact two-parent families. Suppose, for example, that a young man has fathered a child out of wedlock with his girlfriend. If this young father abandons his responsibilities to the mother and child, government will step in and support the mother and child with welfare. If the mother has a second child out of wedlock, as is common, average combined benefits will reach around $13,000 per year.

If, on the other hand, the young man does what society believes is morally correct (marries the mother and takes a job to support his family), government policy takes the opposite course. Welfare benefits are almost completely eliminated, and if the young father makes more than a modest salary, the federal government begins taking away his income through taxes. The federal Welfare Reform Act of 1988 permits the young father to marry the mother and join the family to receive welfare, but only as long as he does not work. Once he takes a full-time job to support his family, welfare benefits are eliminated and the father's earnings are subject to taxation.

Largely because of welfare, illegitimacy and single parenthood have become the conventional "lifestyle option" for raising children in many low-income communities. As *Washington Post* reporter Leon Dash has shown in his book *When Children Want Children*, most unwed teen mothers conceive and deliver their babies deliberately rather than accidentally.[29] While young women do not necessarily bear unwanted children in order to reap windfall profits from welfare, they are very much aware of the role welfare will play in supporting them once a child is born. Thus, the availability of welfare plays an important role in influencing a woman's decision to have a child out of wedlock.

Scientific research confirms that welfare benefits to single mothers contribute directly to the rise in illegitimate births. Research by Dr. C.R. Winegarden of the University of Toledo found that half of the increases in black illegitimacy in recent decades could be attributed to the effects of welfare.[30] Research by Mikhail Bernstam of the Hoover Institution at Stanford University shows that childbearing by young unmarried women may increase by 6 percent in response to a 10 percent increase in monthly welfare benefits; among blacks, the increase may be as high as 10 percent.[31]

Another study of black Americans by Dr. Mark Fossett and Dr. Jill Kiecolt finds that higher welfare benefits lead to lower rates of marriage and greater numbers of children living in single-parent homes:

- In general, in the Fossett study, an increase of roughly $100 in the average monthly AFDC benefit per recipient child was found to lead to a drop of more than 15 percent in births within wedlock among black women ages 20 to 24.[32]
- Research by Shelley Lundberg and Robert D. Plotnick of the University of Washington shows that an increase of roughly $200 per month in welfare benefits per family causes the teenage illegitimate birth rate in a state to increase by 150 percent.[33]
- Dr. June O'Neill's research has found that, holding constant a wide range of other variables such as income, parental education, and urban and neighborhood setting, a 50 percent increase in the monthly value of AFDC and food stamp benefits leads to a 43 percent increase in out-of-wedlock births.[34]
- Research by Dr. Martha Ozawa of Washington University in St. Louis shows somewhat lower but still strong effects: An increase in AFDC benefit levels of $100 per child per month leads to roughly a 30 percent increase in out-of-wedlock births to women age 19 and under.[35]
- Similarly, high benefits discourage single mothers from remarrying. Research by Dr. Robert Hutchens of Cornell University shows that a 10 percent increase in AFDC benefits in a state will cause a decrease in the marriage rate of all single mothers in the state by 8 percent.[36]

The Clinton administration record

President Clinton, at the outset of his presidency, promised "to end welfare as we know it." Unfortunately, the Administration's actions and proposals on welfare contradict the President's public statements. As recently as April 1995, President Clinton stated: "[I]n 1992 I was elected to end welfare as we know it. That was part of my New Covenant of opportunity and responsibility. . . . And I introduced the most sweeping welfare reform the country had ever seen."[37]

Elsewhere, the President has said that "You could not design a program that would be too tough on work for me."[38] But the welfare reform bill the President submitted to Congress had the following characteristics:

- Virtually no welfare recipient was required to work.
- There were no time limits on welfare.
- Only 7 percent of the AFDC caseload was required to work even by 1999.
- Even the small number of recipients required to work were required to do so only for a few hours per week.
- WORK (the name of the new work program) participants were to be paid an effective wage rate of $16.00 per hour.
- The bill limited useful work and the filling of government job openings with former welfare recipients.
- The minimum work requirements were wrongly targeted at the mothers of pre-school children rather than the mothers of children at school. (This provision expanded the welfare system to provide child care to these mothers of young children.) The administrative cost alone for running each WORK person was $4,000.[39]

The President's plan, called the Work and Responsibility Act of 1994, turned out to be more public relations than reform; if enacted, like so many other welfare reform measures of the past, it would do nothing but forestall serious systemic change of America's welfare system. When the rhetoric is removed, the Clinton Administration plan represents little more than a continuing rapid expansion of the current destructive system.[40]

Congress passes a bill

The 104th Congress passed a significant reform of America's failed welfare system based on three themes:

- Reducing the growth of illegitimacy;
- Reducing dependence by requiring welfare recipients to work; and
- Limiting the elements of reform in the legislation.

Among the many elements of reform in the measure, seven are crucial:

1. The bill ends the automatic entitlement nature of AFDC spending, with states that increase their welfare caseloads no longer rewarded by an automatic increase in federal funding. This change imposes a fundamental fiscal discipline at the state level that is essential to real reform.

2. The bill establishes a family cap. Mothers already enrolled in AFDC will not receive an automatic increase in federal benefits if they give birth to an additional child while on welfare. (However, states will be permitted to enact legislation to "opt out" of this requirement.)

3. The bill provides a funding mechanism to reward states which reduce out-of-wedlock births without increasing abortions.

4. The bill provides $75 million per year for a new block grant for abstinence education.

5. For the first time in the history of AFDC, the bill establishes serious work requirements for welfare recipients. Up to 40 percent of the AFDC caseload will be required to work or become self-sufficient by the year 2002. Unlike all previous work requirements in the AFDC program, those in this legislation are real. Recipients who do not obtain private-sector jobs will be required to perform community service in exchange for benefits according to a "pay after performance" rule. Recipients will not receive benefits until the required work has been performed satisfactorily. If they fail to perform the required hours of work, benefits will be reduced pro-rata.

6. The bill properly recognizes that the goal of workfare is to reduce welfare dependence and welfare caseloads, not to maximize the number of welfare recipients in make-work public service jobs. It recognizes that the best road to self-sufficiency is to reduce the number of persons who become dependent on welfare in the first place. Unlike President Clinton's plan, which rewards states for expanding welfare addiction, Congress for the first time focuses on rewarding states that reduce the number of individuals who get hooked on welfare.

7. The bill establishes a firm time limit for receipt of federal AFDC funds; an individual may receive federal AFDC aid for not more than five years. States may exempt 15 percent of the AFDC caseload from this limit.

The President vetoed this welfare reform legislation.

Tax Relief for Families. In tandem with comprehensive welfare reform, Members of Congress have recognized the need to reward work, especially among lower- and middle-income families. Congress thus enacted a $500-per-child tax credit in its balanced budget package. For the average family with two children, that is a significant break, as Table 1 shows. President Clinton vetoed this legislation.

Table 1. What the $500-per-Child Tax Credit Means for a Family with Two Children

Family Budget Item	Annual Household Cost for a Family of Four	Monthly Cost	Number of Months $1,000 Will Purchase
Groceries	$3,986	$332	3.0
Mortgage Payment (Principal, Interest & Taxes)	7,972	664	1.5
Natural Gas	333	28	36.0
Electricity	1,085	90	11.1
Telephone	803	67	14.9
Water	331	28	36.3
Children's Clothing	612	51	19.6
Auto Payments	3,325	277	3.6
Gasoline Purchases	1,397	116	8.6
Health Insurance	817	68	14.7
Medical Services	749	62	16.0
Drugs and Medical Supplies	366	31	32.8
Personal Care Products & Services	526	44	22.8
Educational Expenses	739	62	16.2
Life and Other Personal Insurance	557	46	21.5
Personal Services (Babysitting, Child Care, etc.)	536	45	22.4

Source: Heritage calculations, based on Bureau of Labor Statistics, Consumer Expenditure Survey, 1992–93.

Changes in the Earned Income Tax Credit. The 104th Congress affirmed the continuing expansion of the EITC enacted in previous years, passing a budget which would have raised the basic EITC rate for a working family with two children from 36 percent of earnings in 1995 to 40 percent in 1996.

Congress correctly rescinded Clinton's 1993 expansion of EITC coverage to individuals who were not parents. Single persons who work full-time at the minimum wage automatically have incomes above the poverty level; expanding the EITC to include single persons therefore was both expensive and inappropriate.

Congress did change the EITC formula for parents with children so that the value of the credit would phase down more quickly as family earnings rose above $18,000 per year. However, parents in this income range also would be eligible for the new $500-per-child tax credit. Overall, under the congressional plan, 95 percent of parents with children would see their incomes rise. President Clinton vetoed these changes.

What to do

Rebuilding the Good Society. The reform of America's welfare system should be animated by a broader social vision. Candidates running for the presidency and the Congress should be clear, in this area, about what kind of society they wish to see for current and future generations of Americans. This vision of the better life should not be confined simply to the need to reform public assistance to low-income Americans. It extends to the broader society. The chief object of conservative social policy should be nothing less than the restoration and support of the traditional two-parent family. The traditional family is the foundation of American society: the principal social institution by which the work ethic, self-discipline, intellectual motivation, and moral character are passed on to the next generation. When the family is weakened, the nation is weakened.

For decades the federal government has pursued policies which promote the collapse of the family. Vast changes are required in a wide range of social and welfare policies. These changes should include reducing the government's financial burden on middle-class families with children; reforming welfare to control costs and require work; promoting policies to reduce illegitimacy and thereby improve the quality of life for America's children; reforming divorce law and strengthening marriage; and revitalizing the institutions of civil society.

The traditional family is the original department of health, education, and welfare. But for several decades the government has pursued policies which discourage marriage and make it difficult for the traditional family to carry out its functions. In 1950, the median family of four paid just 3 percent of its income to the federal government in taxes. Today that figure has risen to 24 percent; when state and local taxes are thrown in, the total is even higher: 38 percent.

Reforming welfare to require work and control costs. A considerable portion of those taxes supports a welfare system which, with its huge costs and harmful consequences, requires immediate and drastic reform. Since most of the funding for the current system is provided at the federal level, it follows that the basic structure of reform should occur at the national level. Reform should promote individual responsibility by converting welfare from a one-way handout into a system in which recipients are expected to contribute something for temporary aid received. In addition, it must be undergirded by firm budgetary controls on the growth of future spending. Welfare bureaucracies are prolific in inventing new programs which allegedly promote self-sufficiency but accomplish nothing or actually draw more people into dependence. Without definite limits on the amount of money flowing into this system, such counterproductive "reforms" are difficult to block.

The extraordinary cost of financing the Great Society and the War on Poverty has been borne largely by the middle class, especially parents with children. In response to this crushing tax burden, many in the middle class have delayed marriage and, when they have married, have put off having children, reducing the number of those they do raise. Ironically, even as it discourages child rearing by traditional middle-class families, government aggressively subsidizes child rearing by never-married women who generally are ill-prepared to act as parents. The results of this disastrous policy are all too apparent. Any government policy which places punitive and crippling financial burdens on traditional two-parent families while subsidizing illegitimacy is a recipe for eventual social collapse.

Specific policies needed include the following:

Cut taxes on middle-class families with children. The government must realize that healthy families are the foundation of a successful society; it must seek to strengthen marriage as the crucial institution in which future generations of Americans will be raised. The most obvious step it can take in this regard is to reduce dramatically the current crippling tax burden it places on young working and middle-class parents with children.

The $500-per-child tax credit passed by the Congress and vetoed by President Clinton is only a first step. This tax credit should be enacted now and followed in the near future by larger tax cuts for families with children.

Cap the growth of welfare spending. No matter how frequently policymakers supposedly end welfare, the costs continue to rise. Welfare absorbed around 1.5 percent of GNP when Lyndon Johnson launched the War on Poverty in 1965; it rose to over 5 percent by 1993. With a $324 billion price tag, welfare spending now amounts to $8,300 for each poor person in the U.S. Worse, Congressional Budget Office figures show total welfare costs rising to $500 billion, about 6 percent of GNP, by 1999. To the Clinton Administration, ending welfare has meant spending even more.

The Clinton Administration [welfare reform] plan represents little more than a continuing rapid expansion of the current destructive system.

The long history of bogus welfare reforms, all of which promised to save money but did not, leads to one obvious conclusion: The only way to limit the growth of welfare spending is to do just that: limit the growth of welfare spending. The entitlement nature of federal welfare programs which permits unlimited automatic spending increases should be repealed, and the future growth of federal means-tested welfare spending (excluding medical programs) should be limited to 3 percent per annum.[41] Most non-medical means-tested programs should be folded into a single welfare block grant to the states, with funding permitted to increase at 3 percent each year.

By slowing the outpouring from the federal welfare spigot, this spending cap would gradually reduce the subsidizing of dysfunctional behavior: dependency, non-work, and illegitimacy. It would send a warning signal to state welfare bureaucracies, most of which, cushioned by a steady and increasing flow of federal funds, have found no reason to grapple with the tough and controversial policies needed to reduce illegitimacy and dependency. With a cap on future federal funds, state governments for the first time would be forced to adopt innovative and aggressive policies to reduce the welfare rolls.

Effective workfare

Establish serious workfare. Although liberals often talk about requiring welfare recipients to work, existing welfare law makes it extremely difficult for states to require this. Similarly, the welfare "reforms" proposed by President Clinton would have made it impossible for states to operate efficient work programs.

Congress should establish serious work requirements for able-bodied recipients in federal welfare programs. The key to successful workfare is the number of welfare recipients who are required to participate. Real reform would require all fathers in the AFDC-UP [Unemployed Parents] program to perform 40 hours of community service work per week. It also would require able-bodied single persons in the food stamp program to work. Finally, half of all single mothers on AFDC should be required to perform community service for benefits by 1999.

Under a serious workfare program, recipients would be required to look for private-sector jobs. If a recipient cannot find a private-sector job, he or she should be required to perform community service in exchange for welfare benefits according to a "pay for performance" rule. Under a "pay for performance" system, the recipient would not receive benefits until the required work had been performed satisfactorily; if the recipient failed to perform the required hours of work, welfare benefits would be reduced pro-rata.

The goal of serious workfare is to reduce welfare dependence and caseloads, not to maximize the number of recipients in make-work public service jobs. A properly designed system must be based on an understanding that the most important effect of any work requirement is to separate recipients who truly need assistance because they cannot find employment from those who do not but are willing to take a free handout if it is offered. Thus, a properly designed workfare program has its greatest impact by dramatically shrinking the number of individuals who apply for welfare in the first place. Serious workfare recognizes that the best road to self-sufficiency is to reduce the number of persons who become dependent and "get hooked" on welfare initially.

Establish sensible workfare priorities. Workfare programs should be efficient and low cost. Workfare should be established first for those who have the least justification for being out of the labor force: able-bodied, non-elderly single persons on welfare, followed by fathers in two-parent families on welfare and absent fathers who fail to pay child support.[42] After workfare has been put in operation for the preceding groups, single mothers on AFDC who do not have pre-school children should be required to work.[43]

High day care expenses mean that putting a single mother with a young child to work in a community service program costs roughly two to three times as much as requiring a mother with an older child to work. Because work programs inevitably operate within fixed budgets, an emphasis on workfare participation by mothers with younger children leads to a sharp reduction in the total number of persons who will be required to work. One little-understood aspect of the debate is that liberals often attempt to focus workfare programs on mothers with very young children precisely because they understand this quickly soaks up available funds and thereby limits the number of recipients required to participate. Liberal welfare advocates also try to undermine the general concept of workfare by claiming that all workfare programs cost more than they save; they promote the least cost-effective programs (that is, those with a heavy emphasis on mothers with young children) precisely for this purpose.

Around half of AFDC single mothers have no pre-school children under age five. Workfare should be imposed on single mothers with children under age five only after most mothers with older children have been required to work. However, if an AFDC mother gave birth to another child after her enrollment in AFDC, that should not exempt her from work requirements even if the child is under age five. This rule is needed to prevent mothers from having additional children to escape the work requirement.

Recognize the limits of job training. A perennial panacea in the welfare debate is that education and job training will enable single mothers to obtain good jobs and become self-sufficient. Unfortunately, despite over three decades of experience, government-run training programs have failed to raise the wage rates of welfare recipients by more than a tiny amount. For example, the U.S. Department of Labor in 1993 completed a controlled scientific evaluation of its massive Job Training Partnership Act (JTPA) program. This evaluation showed that the average hourly wage of female trainees was raised by 3.4 percent; the hourly wages of males were not increased at all.[44]

The chief object of conservative social policy should be nothing less than the restoration and support of the traditional two-parent family.

The failure of government training programs is especially salient given the very low cognitive ability levels of many welfare mothers. A study by Child Trends, Inc., finds that mothers in the Aid to Families with Dependent Children program have significantly lower math and verbal abilities than other women of the same ethnic group who are not enrolled in welfare programs. When all U.S. women are ranked according to basic math and verbal skills, over half of welfare mothers are found to have cognitive skill levels placing them in the bottom 20 percent of the overall population. The study states: "The average aptitude or achievement scores of welfare mothers are significantly below the mean of even the lowest of the occupational classes."[45] Government can do little if anything to alter these cognitive skill levels.

The very low cognitive abilities of welfare mothers, coupled with the impotence of government educational and training programs and the cost of child care, underscore the futility of reform schemes aimed narrowly at making unwed mothers employed and self-sufficient. What is needed is more fundamental change aimed at reducing illegitimacy and restoring marriage. To repeat the basic historical lesson: Raising children is a difficult and expensive task which generally requires the efforts of the mother and father bound by the commitment of marriage. It is very difficult for a single parent to find the time and emotional resources needed to raise a child while also working to support the family. The importance of marriage and the contribution of both parents is intensified in the case of parents with low personal skills and earning capacity.

The well-being of American children requires policy changes that not only will reduce illegitimacy and promote marriage, but also will encourage potential parents to defer childbearing until both the mother and the father have acquired the education, job skills, and personal maturity needed to support a family and nurture their children properly. Above all, it is imperative to eliminate the wide array of programs which subsidize and encourage young, poorly educated girls to have children out of wedlock.

Welfare benefits

Replace food stamps with commodities. A major historic expansion of the welfare state occurred when the food stamp program replaced older aid programs which distributed food commodities directly to the poor. The current food stamp program gives individuals food coupons which they can use to purchase food in stores. Unlike food commodities, food coupons can be sold on the black market and converted into cash. Replacing the older food commodities programs with food coupons was a serious mistake that further encouraged rapid increases in welfare dependence and illegitimacy.

Congress should reverse this mistake. Families on AFDC and other persons receiving food stamps (excluding the elderly and disabled) should be given a carefully selected basket of food commodities in lieu of food stamp coupons. Each basket should be carefully balanced to provide the proper levels of proteins, calories, vitamins, and minerals for the family or individual receiving aid. This policy can ensure that no family receiving aid will be malnourished or hungry. It also can be operated at a lower cost than the current program. Moreover, this policy would eliminate food stamp fraud by restricting the beneficiary's ability to sell food stamps on the black market; there would be little or no black market for the donated commodities.

More important, replacing food stamps with commodities would reduce dependence and out-of-wedlock births by reducing the overall attractiveness of welfare. Assuming that substituting food commodities for food stamps would reduce the consumer "utility" of food benefits by a third and the "utility" of the overall AFDC/food stamp benefit package by 15 percent, it also could reduce illegitimate births by more than 5 percent and the AFDC caseload by over 20 percent.

Limit cash benefits to young unmarried mothers. It has been a tragic mistake for the government to pay money to 14-year-old girls on condition that they have children out of wedlock. The government should begin to address the illegitimacy problem by ending its disastrous policy of giving direct AFDC and food stamp benefits to unmarried young mothers. This almost certainly would lead to a sharp and substantial drop in illegitimacy.

Today's welfare system mainly involves failed attempts to pick up the pieces for an ever-increasing number of individuals who have violated the above rules. But from the perspective of society and the child, to have a baby you cannot support either financially or psychologically is profoundly irresponsible. Government policy not only must stop subsidizing and promoting such irresponsible behavior, but must actively discourage it.

Serious welfare reform must focus on the root behavioral problems of illegitimacy and divorce, not merely on the superficial symptom of welfare dependence. Despite rhetoric pledging to "end welfare as we know it," President Clinton is unwilling to take the serious steps needed to deal with the crisis of illegitimacy. The Clinton Administration seeks to devise schemes to help individuals leave welfare rather than to reduce the self-destructive behavior that led to dependence in the first place. This approach is self-deluding. No array of government programs is going to make a 20-year-old woman who has had one or two children out of wedlock self-sufficient. Nor, despite her best efforts, is that single mother likely to be able to provide a truly healthy emotional environment for her children as they develop.

By paying young women to have children out of wedlock, the present welfare system encourages them in a course of action that in the long term proves self-defeating to the mothers and harmful to both the children and society. Placing millions of single mothers in work and training programs will have little positive effect on society as long as the illegitimate birth rate remains over 30 percent. Congress must go to the heart of the dependency problem by seeking to reduce the number of illegitimate births.

At the same time, government should not abandon all aid to children born out of wedlock; federal AFDC and food stamp funds currently given directly to unwed mothers under age 21 should be converted into block grants to the states. State governments could use the funds to develop innovative policies for assisting teenagers who continue to have children out of wedlock. Such policies could include providing in-kind benefits, promoting adoption and orphanages, or supporting the mothers in tightly supervised group homes; but federal funds should no longer be used to provide direct cash welfare benefits to teen mothers. The limitation on benefits should apply to all children born to unwed mothers age 21 and under one year or more after the date of enactment.

Do not provide increased AFDC and food stamp benefits to mothers who bear additional children while already enrolled in the AFDC program. Under the current welfare system, if a mother enrolled in AFDC bears additional children, she receives an automatic increase in AFDC and food stamp benefits. No other family in America receives an automatic increase in its income by having more children. There is no reason to provide expanded welfare benefits to single mothers who have additional illegitimate children while already dependent on welfare. A limitation of this sort already has been put into effect in the state of New Jersey by Democratic Assemblyman Wayne Bryant. Evidence from controlled scientific experiments designed to determine its effects show a 10 percent decrease in illegitimate births to mothers on AFDC as a result of the family cap.[46]

Require the establishment of paternity for children receiving AFDC. Current law requires that an AFDC mother make a "good faith" effort to identify the father of her child in order to receive AFDC. This law is ignored. The government should require, for children born prospectively, that the mother identify the father in order to receive any federally funded welfare aid.[47] Exceptions to this rule in a few hardship cases could be made, but they should not exceed 10 percent.

It has been a tragic mistake for the government to pay money to 14-year-old girls on condition that they have children out of wedlock.

Modern DNA testing permits determination of a child's real father with absolute confidence. Once the mother has identified the father and paternity has been established, the father can be required to pay child support to offset welfare costs. If the father claims he cannot pay any child support because he cannot find a job, the government may require that he perform community service to fulfill his obligation. Experiments with this approach in Wisconsin have led to surprising increases in the ability of absent fathers to locate private-sector employment and pay child support. Moreover, the definite expectation among young men that they will be identified and required to pay child support for their children may put an end to the ethos in some communities where young men assert their masculinity by fathering children they have no intention of supporting.

Encourage state-based "faith and families" programs. The "faith and families" program created by Mississippi Governor Kirk Fordice is one of the most innovative and interesting welfare reforms in the U.S. today. This program seeks to link single mothers on AFDC with church congregations throughout the state, placing at least one welfare family under the tutelage of each church. The congregation effectively becomes the case worker for the welfare mother, providing mentoring, moral authority, life skills training, and contact with employment opportunities. The recipient continues to receive her welfare check from the government bureaucracy, but most other aspects of managing the case are under church control. The program also is voluntary in that any recipient can choose to have her case handled by welfare bureaucrats rather than a church.

Striking a theme which would have been common in earlier generations but has been painfully absent in American discourse for over half a century, Governor Fordice has declared that "God, not government, will be the savior of welfare recipients." This new policy should be copied in other states.

Reduce government welfare by increasing private-sector charity. There is widespread recognition that government welfare has failed—indeed, that government is the least effective institution in aiding the poor. Yet, each year, hundreds of billions of dollars taken forcibly from the paychecks of Americans are spent on government welfare programs in which the people no longer have confidence.

Real welfare reform will require rechanneling a major portion of current funding into private secular and religious charities rather than government programs. Legislation introduced in 1995 by Representatives Jim Kolbe (R-AZ) and Joseph Knollenberg (R-MI) would permit just that. The Kolbe-Knollenberg bill has three key principles:

- Any taxpayer could give up to $100 to any private charity devoted exclusively to aiding the poor;
- Taxpayers would have their federal taxes reduced by the sum given to charity; and
- Federal welfare spending would be reduced by the same amount.

The bill, in essence, would allow any taxpayer to opt out of the federal welfare system; those who lack confidence in government welfare could divert their money to private charity instead. The taxpayer would be able to choose among a large number of private charities which would compete with one another to demonstrate which was the most effective in aiding the poor. Similar legislation was drafted by Senator Dan Coats (R-IL).

Questions and answers

Why are conservative welfare reforms punishing single parents and their children?

Nothing punishes single parents and their children more than the current welfare system. For millions of children and their parents, this system is the proverbial free ticket to a bus going nowhere. The reason: It is riddled with perverse incentives that discourage work and marriage while encouraging illegitimate birth and long-term dependency. Precisely because single-parent family life is much harder on the children, as well as their mothers and the broader society, it is no kindness for government to make either single parenthood or long-term dependency easier and more common.

Given the perverse incentives of the system, millions of parents and their children cannot escape to a better life, but will be locked instead into more of the same. It is a condition that not only undermines their upward economic mobility and eventual independence, but also robs them of hope for the future and reinforces spiritual despair.

Conservative welfare reform aims to discourage single mothers from having more children out of wedlock while helping them through the transition to a life in which it is economically rational to marry or get a job.

Why do conservatives in Congress want to cut welfare?

Conservatives in Congress are not proposing to cut welfare. Under the Republican proposals aggregate welfare spending on non-medical programs will grow at roughly 4 percent per year.

Liberals in Congress generally oppose serious welfare reform and, as evidenced during the debate on school lunch programs, do not even favor reducing the rate of welfare spending. Total welfare spending in the United States is $324 billion, 72 percent of it federal and 28 percent of it state spending. Moreover, nine-tenths of all state welfare spending amounts to a state contribution to federal programs. At the current rate of spending, assuming nothing is changed, the United States will be spending $500 billion on welfare by the year 1999, or 6 percent of the gross national product (GNP). To put this in perspective, at the current rate, taxpayers will be shelling out $2 in welfare spending for every $1 we now spend on national defense.

Conservatives in Congress simply want to impose some discipline on welfare spending, just as they do in other areas of federal spending. They are prepared to let already high levels of welfare spending grow, but only at some reasonable rate, not at the explosive rate at which it has been growing.

But didn't conservatives in Congress propose to cut school lunch and women, infants, and children (WIC) programs in 1995?

Congressional appropriators attempted to convert the federal school lunch and breakfast programs into a block grant, which would grow at 4.5 percent per year. Liberals complained that the original baseline for growth in the program was 5.1 percent, and thus that reducing the growth in spending amounted to a "cut." It is patently dishonest to call a growth in spending a cut, but even with this modest change, Congress still would be wasting federal funds by providing school lunch subsidies to middle-class families and even to the children of millionaires instead of targeting them exclusively to poor children.

As for WIC, it was not cut. It was folded into a block grant with a few other programs. The money available for WIC, like the money available for school lunches, was to increase. Incredibly, under the traditional WIC program, benefits were available to families earning up to $28,000 per year even though a family in that income range pays about $6,000 per year in federal taxes. Conservative policy for middle-income families is not to give them welfare benefits, but to cut their taxes.

Conservatives in Congress are not proposing to cut welfare.

Won't spending reductions in existing federal welfare programs and block grants jeopardize poor families?

Few, if any, welfare programs have operated as expected, so poor families have not benefited as expected. The largest federal program, Aid to Families with Dependent Children (AFDC), was designed in 1935 to support widows and orphans. Only 1.5 percent of the beneficiaries today are widows and orphans. Instead, AFDC has served as the financial mainstay of single parenthood among low-income persons. Likewise, there are nine different federal jobs and training programs for low-income persons, costing an estimated $5.3 billion.[48] After three decades of federal job training programs, the wage rates of beneficiaries have hardly been affected. A Labor Department study of the impact of the Job Training Partnership Act, for example, showed that female trainees' wages increased by a mere 3.4 percent and that male trainees' wages did not increase at all. Five recent scientific studies of federal jobs programs for poor people showed that none of them worked. Few federal jobs programs ever lead to real, permanent jobs in the private sector.

By combining dozens of federal welfare programs into block grants to the states, eliminating tens of thousands of pages of federal regulations, and letting governors and state legislatures take direct responsibility and do what they think is best for their communities, welfare reform can serve low-income people more efficiently. States and local communities, working with dedicated people in private organizations in these communities, are likely to have the best ideas about what works in preventing teen pregnancy or in setting up day care and jobs programs to help lift poor people out of poverty and dependency.

Helping the poor

If conservatives want to lift low-income families out of poverty, how do they propose to help them?

The best way to keep a mother and her children out of poverty is to help make sure they have a working father with a regular paycheck who comes home every night. Right now, if a young man marries the mother of his child and makes anything over $6.50 per hour, we tax his income. For persons currently on welfare, this does not encourage either marriage or upward economic mobility.

But by making serious tax changes, particularly by giving low-income families generous tax relief, a conservative social policy would reward work, increase disposable family income, and help keep families together. Under Representative Dick Armey's proposal to replace the current tax code with a flat tax, for example, any family of four with an income of $33,000 per year or less would pay no income tax at all.[49] Moreover, by eliminating outdated penalties on savings and investment, conservative tax policies would stimulate more investment and economic growth, and thus create more real jobs, open up new opportunities, and generate higher wages for family breadwinners.

If conservatives in Congress want to help low-income working families, why didn't they support President Clinton's family tax relief proposal rather than pass a balanced budget plan that would gut the popular Earned Income Tax Credit and raise taxes on families earning less than $30,000?

Even after changing the Earned Income Tax Credit, the Balanced Budget Act of 1995, with its $500-per-child tax credit, would benefit 5.4 million more low-income working families with children than the Clinton Administration tax proposal with its $300-per-child tax credit. In fact, the congressional proposal, vetoed by President Clinton, would allow a low-income family to take a $500-per-child tax credit first, and then receive the full value of the EITC on top of the child credit. Under the Clinton plan, a low-income family would have to deduct EITC benefits from income tax before taking the less generous $300-per-child tax credit. Thus, a family with two children would have to earn $24,000 a year before becoming eligible for the Clinton credit. Worse, because the Clinton tax credit is available only to families with children under the age of 13, families are denied tax relief for children precisely when the cost of raising them becomes even more expensive. Under the Clinton tax credit plan, 2.8 million children in families earning less than $30,000 per year would be denied eligibility for tax relief. Under the congressional plan, a family would be eligible for a more generous tax credit at roughly $17,000 a year.

What steps can the government take to reduce illegitimacy?

First, unlike age, disability, or veteran status, illegitimacy should not be the basis of a legal entitlement to a government check. Unwed mothers can and should be assisted in other ways, including the establishment of group homes for unwed mothers or maternity homes. Young men and women may be entitled to a mistake, but taxpayers cannot afford to subsidize further mistakes through automatic increases in benefits to women who continue to have additional children while on welfare.

Second, sexual abstinence programs should be incorporated into welfare reform measures, particularly at the state level. The data show that such programs work,[50] much as the Just Say No campaigns against illegal drugs in the 1980s worked. Teenagers are not stupid. They can see the difference between a young man's lifelong commitment to the mother and their baby and the momentary enjoyment of sexual pleasure with life-changing consequences and without the commitment of marriage. All the proposals to make marriage more attractive also help to reduce illegitimacy.

Third, it is time to get serious about cracking down on statutory rape. In a significant percentage of illegitimacy cases, the mother is well below the age of consent and the father is in his mid-twenties. It is past time that such adult males, taking advantage of teenage girls, face charges of rape.

Fourth, toughen child support enforcement. Policymakers should inflict financial pain on men who sire children and then abandon the mothers. Men should be made to take responsibility for the upbringing of their children. Tough enforcement of child support also helps get the message across that the costs of illegitimacy must be borne by the father as much as by the child and mother.

Unlike age, disability, or veteran status, illegitimacy should not be the basis of a legal entitlement to a government check.

But don't congressional conservatives want to consign poor children to orphanages?

For neglected, unwanted, or physically or sexually abused children, state or local authorities might determine that an orphanage is not an unreasonable solution. In some cases, it is the only viable option. And, regardless of the negative images conjured up by liberal opponents, sound policy should include this possibility. While Hillary Rodham Clinton ridiculed the concept as "absurd," under persistent questioning from Representative Bill Archer of Texas, Chairman of the House Ways and Means Committee, Health and Human Services (HHS) Secretary Donna Shalala admitted that even under the Clinton Administration welfare plan, orphanages would be an option.

Aren't conservatives expecting too much of private charities when the government cuts back on the spending increases in social services?

Not at all. First, under real welfare reform, with new incentives to work and get off the welfare rolls, there will be a drop in the welfare rolls even as there is a simultaneous increase in total welfare spending. In other words, there will be more money, rather than less, for those in need. Second, under the congressional block grant approach, state and local governments will work directly with local charitable organizations, not only to provide social services, but also to help poor people become self-sufficient.

States that have introduced serious work requirements for welfare recipients have registered significant drops in the welfare rolls ranging from 50 to 90 percent.

After decades of painful experience, Congress and the federal bureaucracy must admit that neither they nor the programs they have designed over the past half century have been effective in reducing the welfare rolls, curbing illegitimacy, or making low-income Americans economically independent.

Beyond the promise of welfare reform, Congress can assist private charities even more directly in helping the poor. Senator Daniel Coats (R-IN), for example, has introduced a bill that would allow a tax credit of as much as $1,000 for donations to charities that directly help the needy poor. This will increase the ability of charities to help these people.

Won't conservative cuts in social programs increase the number of hungry children? HHS says that over 1 million people will be thrown into poverty.

The HHS study is flawed. It assumes that the conservative congressional reforms, just like the several previous—and notoriously unsuccessful—liberal attempts to "end welfare as we know it," will fail and that welfare rolls will continue to increase at about 3 percent per annum. But there are dramatic differences, both in assumptions and in policies, between liberal and conservative welfare reforms.

In the past, liberals have attempted to make the welfare system work. For the future, conservatives want to make welfare recipients work. Conservative policies can assume a decrease in the welfare rolls precisely because they introduce serious work requirements into welfare reform. For example, in dealing with married AFDC families, states that have introduced serious work requirements for welfare recipients have registered significant drops in the welfare rolls ranging from 50 to 90 percent.

In speaking of the HHS study, American Enterprise Institute Senior Fellow Ben J. Wattenberg remarked that "The assumptions of these studies strangely do not take into account the very purpose of the bill—to encourage young people to have children after marriage, not before, thus sharply improving children's economic circumstances. Studies that assume welfare reform will not work are the work of those who believe that welfare reform will not work. Hence, the studies are useless and misleading." [51]

Notes:

1. Robert Rector and William F. Lauber, *America's Failed $5.4 Trillion War on Poverty* (Washington, D.C.: The Heritage Foundation, 1995), Appendix One.

2. This section is adapted from *ibid.*, Chapter Two.

3. Historical spending data used here and other historical social statistics may be found in *ibid.*, Appendix Two.

4. Clearly, not all persons in the lowest income quartile will receive welfare benefits, and some benefits will go to individuals in higher income groups. Overall, however, a reasonable estimate would put the total number of recipients of means-tested aid at about one quarter of the U.S. population. Thus, Charts 3 and 4 give a reasonably accurate picture of welfare spending relative to the recipient population.

5. For purposes of consistency, federal means-tested education aid is included with welfare spending in the comparison. This sum equaled $17.3 billion in 1993, or 5 percent of total welfare spending; shifting these funds out of welfare and into education would not materially affect the comparison in Chart 6.

6. For purposes of consistency, Medicare spending on poor persons has been included in the welfare category rather than in the Medicare category. See the discussion under Medicare in Rector and Lauber, *America's Failed $5.4 Trillion War on Poverty*, Appendix One. This sum amounted to $15.5 billion in 1993; it represents 4 percent of combined Medicare and Social Security payments and 5 percent of total welfare spending. Shifting it from the welfare category to the Social Security and Medicare category would not significantly affect the comparison in Chart 6.

7. The cost of military production and military and civilian personnel in World War II was $315 billion (in 1940s prices). See Alan S. Milward, *War, Economy and Society: 1939–1945* (Berkeley and Los Angeles: University of California Press, 1979), p. 64. Slightly lower war cost figures are provided in U.S. Bureau of the Census, *Historical Statistics of the United States, Colonial Times to 1970, Bicentennial Edition, Part 2* (Washington, D.C.: U.S. Government Printing Office, 1975), p. 1114.

8. The figure on business infrastructure in Chart 8 equals the net value of tangible non-residential fixed assets in private-sector business and industry in 1993. The figure includes the value of all plant, structure, and equipment in the following industries: all manufacturing, all construction, all transportation, all utilities, all communications, all mining, all wholesale trade, all retail trade, all business real estate, all hotels and lodging, and all other service industries. Agriculture, forestry, and fisheries have not been included. See U.S. Department of Commerce, Bureau of Economic Analysis, *Survey of Current Business*, August 1994, p.55.

9. The text refers to the net value of all buildings, equipment, and vehicles in business sectors mentioned. The actual purchase price of a given firm could be lower or higher than the value of its tangible plant and equipment based on intangible factors such as expected future earnings. See *ibid.*, Table 2.

10. Robert Rector, "How the Poor Really Live: Lessons for Welfare Reform," Heritage Foundation *Backgrounder* No. 875, January 31, 1992. See also

Robert Rector, "Facts About America's Poor," Heritage Foundation *F.Y.I.* No. 6, December 23, 1993.

11. Robert Rector, Kate Walsh O'Beirne, and Michael McLaughlin, "How Poor Are America's Poor?" Heritage Foundation *Backgrounder* No. 791, September 21, 1990, p. 2.

12. Robert Rector, "Food Fight: How Hungry Are America's Children?" *Policy Review*, Fall 1991, pp. 38–43; Robert Rector, "Hunger and Malnutrition Among American Children," Heritage Foundation *Backgrounder* No. 843, August 2, 1991.

13. Bernard D. Karpinos, *Height and Weight of Military Youths* (Medical Statistics Division, Office of the Surgeon General, Department of the Army, 1960), pp. 336–351. Information on the current height and weight of youths provided by the National Center for Health Statistics of the U.S. Department of Health and Human Services, based on the National Health and Nutrition Examination Survey.

14. Rector, "How the Poor Really Live," pp. 12–13.

15. *Ibid.*

16. This sum equals the value of welfare benefits from different programs for the average mother on AFDC.

17. Technically, the mother may be married to a husband who works part-time at very low wages and still be eligible for some aid under the AFDC-UP (Unemployed Parents) program. However, if the husband works a significant number of hours per month, even at a low hourly rate, his earnings will be sufficient to eliminate the family's eligibility for AFDC and most other welfare.

18. One simplistic solution to the dilemmas presented above would be to allow a welfare mother to retain all or most of her welfare benefits after she has taken a job or married a fully employed male. But this approach would be unfair to working single mothers and low-income working married couples who never went on welfare in the first place. Moreover, low- and moderate-income parents would have a huge incentive to enroll in welfare, at least briefly, to become eligible for the long-term continuing benefits. Such a system would devolve inevitably into one in which the majority of low- and moderate-income single- and two-parent families received substantial welfare payments, raising the overall cost of welfare by hundreds of billions of dollars per year. Realistic welfare reformers must seek to alter welfare incentives in a more practical manner.

19. Committee on Ways and Means, *1993 Green Book: Background Materials and Data on Programs within the Jurisdiction of the Committee on Ways and Means* (Washington, D.C.: U.S. Government Printing Office, 1993), p. 714.

20. M. Anne Hill and June O'Neill, *Underclass Behaviors in the United States: Measurement and Analysis of Determinants* (New York: City University of New York, Baruch College, March 1990).

21. U.S. Bureau of the Census, Current Population Reports, Series P-60, No. 80, *Income in 1970 of Families and Persons in the United States*, p. 26.

22. U.S. Bureau of the Census, Current Population Reports, Series P-60, No. 180, *Money Income of Households, Families and Persons in the United States: 1991*, p. 7.

23. SRI International, *Final Report of the Seattle-Denver Income Maintenance Experiment, Vol. 1, Design and Results* (Washington, D.C.: SRI, May 1983).

24. Gregory B. Christiansen and Walter E. Williams, "Welfare Family Cohesiveness and Out of Wedlock Births," in Joseph Peden and Fred Glahe, *The American Family and the State* (San Francisco: Pacific Institute for Public Policy Research, 1986), p. 398.

25. Charles Murray, *Losing Ground: American Social Policy from 1950 to 1980* (New York: Basic Books, 1984), p. 151.

26. M. Anne Hill and June O'Neill, *Underclass Behaviors in the United States: Measurement and Analysis of Determinants* (New York: City University of New York, Baruch College, August 1993), research funded by Grant No. 88ASPE201A, U.S. Department of Health and Human Services.

27. *Ibid.*

28. U.S. Department of Health and Human Services, National Center for Health Statistics. The black illegitimate birth rate is available only from 1969; pre-1969 rates were calculated using the very similar "non-white" rate.

29. Leon Dash, *When Children Want Children: An Inside Look at the Crisis of Teenage Parenthood* (Penguin Books, 1990).

30. C.R. Winegarden, "AFDC and Illegitimacy Ratios: A Vector Autoregressive Model," *Applied Economics*, March 1988, pp. 1589–1601.

31. Mikhail S. Bernstam, "Malthus and Evolution of the Welfare State: An Essay on the Second Invisible Hand, Parts I and II," Working Papers E-88-41, 42 (Palo Alto: Hoover Institution, 1988).

32. Mark A. Fossett and K. Jill Kiecolt, "Mate Availability and Family Structure Among African Americans in U.S. Metropolitan Areas," *Journal of Marriage and Family*, Vol. 55 (May 1993), pp. 288–302.

33. Shelley Lundberg and Robert D. Plotnick, "Adolescent Premarital Childbearing: Do Opportunity Costs Matter?" June 1990, a revised version of a paper presented at the May 1990 Population Association of America Conference in Toronto, Canada.

34. Hill and O'Neill, *Underclass Behaviors in the United States*, August 1993.

35. Other studies which find a relationship between higher welfare benefits and increased illegitimacy include Charles Murray, "Welfare and the Family: The U.S. Experience," *Journal of Labor Economics*, Vol. 11, No. 1, Pt. 2 (1993), pp. 224–262; Paul T. Schultz, "Marital Status and Fertility in the United States," *The Journal of Human Resources*, Spring 1994, pp. 637–659; Scott J. South and Kim M. Lloyd, "Marriage Markets and Nonmarital Fertility in the United States," *Demography*, May 1992, pp. 247–264; Phillip K. Robins and Paul Fronstin, "Welfare Benefits and Family Size Decisions of Never-Married Women," *Institute for Research on Poverty Discussion Paper*, DP #1022–93, September 1993; Catherine A. Jackson and Jacob Alex Klerman, "Welfare, Abortion and Teenage Fertility," RAND research paper, August 1994.

36. Robert Hutchens, "Welfare, Remarriage, and Marital Search," *American Economic Review*, June 1989, pp. 369–379.

37. Remarks by the President to the American Society of Newspaper Editors, Dallas, Texas, April 7, 1995.

38. Remarks by the President at NGA National Summit on Young Children, Baltimore, Maryland, June 6, 1995.

39. For further detail, see Robert Rector, "How Clinton's Bill Extends Welfare as We Know It," Heritage Foundation *Issue Bulletin No. 200*, August 1, 1994.

40. *Ibid.*, p. 1.

41. Medicaid and means-tested veterans programs should be exempted from the cap.

42. For example, modest work requirements on males in the food stamp program have been shown to reduce welfare rolls significantly, cutting welfare costs by nearly a third and immediately saving several dollars in welfare expenditures for every dollar spent operating the work program. See data on the San Diego food stamp workfare program in U.S. Department of Agriculture, Food and Nutrition Service, Office of Analysis and Evaluation, *Food Stamp Work Registration and Job Search Demonstration: Final Report*, Contract No. 53-3198-0-85, July 1986, pp. 169, 251.

43. There should be no blanket two-year exemption from work requirements. Work requirements which are imposed when a recipient initially enrolls in welfare are likely to have the strongest possible effect in reducing welfare rolls because they dissuade individuals from enrolling in welfare in the first place. Thus, serious work requirements mandated at the time of initial welfare enrollment are likely to be the most cost-effective workfare programs.

44. U.S. Department of Labor, Employment and Training Administration, *The National JTPA Study: Title II-A Impacts on Earnings and Employment at 18 Months*, Research and Evaluation Report 93-C, 1993.

45. Nicholas Zill, Kristin Moore, Christine Ward, and Thomas Stief, *Welfare Mothers as Potential Employees: A Statistical Profile Based on National Survey Data*, Child Trends, Inc. (2100 M Street, N.W., Suite 610, Washington, D.C. 20037), February 25, 1991.

46. Robert Rector, "New Jersey Experiment Sharply Cuts Illegitimate Births Among Welfare Mothers," Heritage Foundation *F.Y.I.* No. 50, February 9, 1995.

47. For children born years ago, it often is impossible to locate the father. The paternity establishment rule therefore should be applied prospectively: The mother should be required to establish paternity in order to receive welfare for children born in 1995 and after.

48. Rector and Lauber, *America's Failed $5.4 Trillion War on Poverty*, p. 39.

49. See Daniel J. Mitchell, "Which Tax Reform Plan Is Best for America?" Heritage Foundation *Backgrounder* No. 1055, September 26, 1995.

50. See Joseph J. Piccione and Robert A. Scholle, "Combatting Illegitimacy and Counseling Teen Abstinence: A Key Component of Welfare Reform," Heritage Foundation *Backgrounder* No. 1051, August 31, 1995.

51. Ben J. Wattenberg, "Welfare Whispers: Will Clinton Hang Tough?" *The Washington Times*, November 9, 1995, p. A17.

6

Welfare Reform Should Emphasize Family Unity

Karl Zinsmeister

Karl Zinsmeister is the editor in chief of the American Enterprise *magazine, a bimonthly publication of the American Enterprise Institute, a public policy research organization in Washington, D.C.*

Despite presidential promises to reform welfare, the number of welfare recipients has reached a record high—almost twenty million Americans at an annual cost of hundreds of billions of dollars. Current welfare-reform strategies that mandate public employment will not be effective because welfare recipients lack the skills and work ethic to become productive and governments lack the discipline to ensure worker effectiveness. Rather than focusing on providing income to support single mothers, welfare reform should encourage marriage among the poor and should strive to keep two-parent families intact.

At this point, it's almost a kabuki ritual. Driven by public distress, leaders in Washington promise "major reform" of the welfare system. They pledge to "turn the public assistance system upside down." They swear they'll "end welfare as we know it."

Each of the last eight presidents has promised salvation. Lyndon Johnson declared War on Poverty. Richard Nixon promised to end all problems with a "guaranteed income." Ronald Reagan pledged dramatic reform, then settled for a pitiful "work incentive" refinement. The year 1988 brought the "Family Support Act" and ballyhooed expectations of transforming welfare into a wholesome job program. It's a twice-a-decade Washington habit. It's a ghastly cicada that emerges from the earth every five or six years, singing a siren song, only to sneak back into the deep after achieving its selfish purposes—with the world left behind utterly unimproved by its presence.

Only one thing has been accomplished by this miserable repeating cycle of sham welfare reforms: Time and again, there has been an ineffectual venting of public determination to see our current, corrosive welfare edifice dismantled. The actual number of individuals languishing on

Karl Zinsmeister, "Chance of a Lifetime," *American Enterprise*, January/February 1995. Reprinted by permission of the *American Enterprise*, a Washington, D.C.–based magazine of business, politics, and culture.

our welfare rolls as squalid dependents, meanwhile, has risen to an historic high—*nearly 20 million souls, in all.* Whole generations of Americans have grown up without any experience of independence and personal responsibility. Amidst the human wreckage strewn glaringly across our national landscape, the annual financial costs to taxpayers of hundreds of billions of dollars seem only a comparatively modest part of the problem.

Given welfare reform's recent history as an intellectual and political cul-de-sac, I startle even myself as I prepare to write my next thought: A dramatic redirection of the U.S. welfare system—and no mere tinkering—is today within reach.

Even before reform Republicans crested into Congress in November 1994, many of us who ached to see our current cruel system of welfare addiction broken up felt that the chances of genuine reform might be better than at any time since the launching of the War on Poverty 30 years previously. After all, President Bill Clinton owed his election to one bold promise to be the Democrat who would eliminate welfare in its current forms. (This had the same public appeal as hiring the Dirty Dozen to clean up Tombstone.)

Meanwhile, Daniel Patrick Moynihan, the original sentinel of welfare-linked social decay, had unexpectedly been installed—in one of those delicious turns of history where whipping boy is elevated to master—as chairman of the Senate Finance Committee, the veritable War Room of welfare policy. Moynihan subsequently devoted much of 1993 and 1994 to insistent prodding of president and adjutants not to neglect their welfare-transformation stepchild.

Most of the long-term, hard-core recipients who represent welfare's real problem population will make abysmal employees.

More fundamentally, an American public jolted by a crack epidemic and crime wave, sobered by recurrent urban unrest, and deeply troubled by a runaway illegitimacy curve was suddenly in no mood for liberal social theory. Indicator lights glowed all across the nation. Even the normally apologetic *Washington Post* splashed an unflinching eight-part series on welfare pathology across its front pages in the fall of 1994, withering the overseers and dishonest clients of our current welfare system with equal censure.

Then came the Great Revolt Against the State, and the election of a venturous troop of progressivists presworn to sharp departures in welfare policy. Suddenly all the meters of political unthinkability cry out for recalibration.

Great social reforms, like most forms of human development, tend to occur in fits and leaps rather than gradual increments. After decades of increasingly unwholesome decay, it is possible we are now approaching one of those rare alignments of the cultural planets where conventional constraints on problem-solving and social invention need not bind.

Among other innovations, real solutions to the wrenching tragedy of America's underclass could follow.

Workfare will not work

And yet . . .

The glistening opportunity may still be squandered.

For the truth is, the welfare reform strategy that currently ranks as the glib favorite in Washington and many state capitols (where much of the real action will take place) is a disastrous dead end. I am referring to the combination of "workfare" rules and new daycare entitlements that lie at the heart of President Clinton's 1994 welfare reform plan and many of the other proposals with which it competes.

As [attorney and writer] George Liebmann has written elsewhere, the Clintonite proposals are neither fresh nor even particularly relevant. "The core of the bill is a scheme, similar to many fostered since the Nixon administration, to drive a small percentage of welfare mothers into the workforce and their children into publicly supported daycare centers, for which several billion dollars are sought to be appropriated—essentially a feminist agenda rather than a welfare reform one."

The workfare+daycare path holds no promise whatever. It is, indeed, nothing more than an expansion of what we already have (the 1988 welfare reform was also billed as workfare salvation). There is an admitted appeal to the idea of trading relief checks for work. But the actual practice of government workfare has no resemblance at all to what the public has in mind when it envisions that simple work-for-aid swap. For two reasons:

First, governments and government-supervised workplaces exhibit relatively little discipline. Even using smart, healthy, well-paid workers—three-quarters of a million of them—the government can barely get the mail delivered. Imagine the efficiency of a government office or worksite staffed by welfare mothers.

Which brings us to the second flaw in workfare, namely that most of the long-term, hard-core recipients who represent welfare's real problem population will make abysmal employees. The idea that you can turn these women into nice middle-class workers by running them through a few perfunctory job training classes (just how perfunctory can only be believed by sitting through some) is ludicrous. According to a 1994 Columbia University study, four out of every ten welfare mothers are serious drug abusers. Most of them are miserably educated. The vast majority have deep emotional problems. Most have small children to take care of. These women have no work experience, no work habits, few basic disciplines. The hard reality seen in scores of programs is that simply getting them out of bed in the morning can be a major challenge.

This is why the Congressional Budget Office has estimated it will cost $3,300 just to provide basic monitoring for each workfare enrollee. On top of that you have to add a huge bill for training just to instill marginal office or manual skills, plus the cost of tools, supplies, and workstations, plus the expense of daycare for the children, plus the amount of the welfare grant. Soon you find that it costs governments a mountain of money to keep these individuals occupied, that most produce very little for it, and that their effective pay rates approach $16 per hour on the job. That isn't likely to hurry too many people away from welfare dependence.

The theory, again, is that the welfare recipients will eventually get *real* jobs and live happily ever after in ranch houses. The reality isn't even close. After seven years, the 1988 workfare bill has resulted in less than 1 percent of all welfare recipients going to work, despite $13 billion in extra expenditures. The most optimistic projections in President Clinton's proposal promised that $9.2 billion in extra spending over five years will induce 6 percent of the total welfare population to participate in "work programs."

In terms of actual individuals, the rosy scenario in the original Clinton plan projects that new workfare rules would nudge 70,000 parents off the welfare rolls by the turn of the century, and 130,000 more into "subsidized jobs." Sounds OK, until you realize there are currently close to 15 million individuals receiving AFDC [Aid to Families with Dependent Children]. Until you notice that the increased costs necessary to induce this work would amount to something like $50 billion. Until you notice the projections showing that while these few adults trickle off welfare and into jobs, 450,000 new households will go onto welfare for the first time, due to continuing family breakdown.

We actually don't have to guess about the likely effects of workfare + daycare efforts, because since 1981 well-developed test programs have been underway in places like Baltimore, San Diego, Arkansas, and Virginia. Careful studies of these pilot projects find workfare sadly inadequate. In the very best programs, the average increase in individual earnings per year thanks to workfare totals between $100 and $500—not exactly the foundation for a brave new world of financial independence. Eighty-two percent of all workfare participants are still on public assistance a year-and-a-half after entering their program, according to a 1994 study by the Manpower Demonstration Research Corporation. In addition, more than half of all welfare mothers become pregnant again out of wedlock after starting workfare.

Restoring family ties

If not workfare, then what?

The vastly superior alternative is, to put it in simple terms, family restoration. The only way to solve our welfare problem and the harsh social fallout it produces is to focus much more on preventing nonworkable single-parent families from forming in the first place. In the future we need to scramble in creative new ways to get low-income mothers and fathers married. We need cultural and economic encouragements to keep parents together in peaceful, intact homes. We need legal changes to discourage divorce and abandonment. In particular, we need measures to reduce the number of illegitimate births—because unmarried mothers are statistically much poorer, less mature, less likely to enter the workforce, and more likely to do a deficient job of raising their children than others.

Changes like these—focusing on family ties instead of income— would represent truly effective welfare reform. Workfare+daycare strategies, on the other hand, not only will fail to work as advertised, they actually address the wrong problem. The inadequacy of the single-parent home as a childrearing and economic unit is not going to be cured by artificially bolstering it with daycare and job services. Instead, the solution is to work to make the single-parent family scarce.

The first step to that goal is ending public financial aid that is conditioned on illegitimacy. We should stop increasing payments to current AFDC recipients when they have additional births out of wedlock. We should phase out for all future applicants any AFDC payments to unmarried mothers. We should instead enforce the legal responsibilities of fathers and relatives, and the liability of parents to support minor daughters who have babies. We should generously fund a string of new and expanded privately run maternity homes, in all shapes and flavors. We should make a giant effort to assist the adoption into loving homes of children whose parents can't or won't raise them. For a small number of hard-to-adopt or abandoned older children we should establish some progressive group homes and orphanages (for "social orphans" instead of the mortality orphans of the past)—modeled on highly successful and humane institutions like Boys Town and the Milton Hershey School.

The only way to solve our welfare problem . . . is to focus much more on preventing nonworkable single-parent families from forming in the first place.

In the words of *Washington Post* and *New Republic* writer Charles Krauthammer, "Don't reform welfare. Don't reinvent it. When it comes to illegitimacy, abolish it. . . . Two years and out, however well intentioned, misses the point. The point is to root out at its origin the most perverse government incentive program of all: The subsidy for illegitimacy. Why? Because illegitimacy is the royal road to poverty and all its attendant pathologies. . . . The only realistic way to attack this cycle . . . is by cutting off the oxygen that sustains the system: Stop the welfare checks."

We have no illusion as to the sufficiency of the average welfare candidate left to her own devices. That is why much of the [January/February 1995] issue of the *American Enterprise* [where this viewpoint originally appeared] is devoted to practical suggestions and models for nongovernmental charitable efforts that can, and would, step into the breach. Such ventures would actually provide individuals with much more benevolent forms of assistance, in a new world of sharply reduced government welfare.

Forswearing the disastrous miscalculations of existing welfare policy will take some nerve. But it will not require any foolhardy leap into dangerous unscouted territory. There were good works being done and lives being redirected in this country long before we had an overweening welfare apparatus. There may have been as much poverty in those days, but there was not nearly so much hopelessness. Given less suffocating competition from the state, these good works will once again be carried out in great number by a riotous parade of public but nongovernmental groups.

The issue, then, is comparatively simple: Do we have the imagination and confidence to re-envision such a world? And do our elected representatives have the requisite courage and wit to force the necessary innovations through the dead resistance of political selfishness and bureaucratic inertia? A much healthier future beckons. But getting there will require something akin to a national narcotic withdrawal. It won't be easy even if all the right and brave decisions are made. So the question becomes—how badly do we want to go clean?

We are not likely to get a better chance any time soon. And how we respond may dictate how Americans of the twenty-first century ultimately view our era. Will they look back and see a handful of decades when some frightening social disorders burgeoned and then faded away? Or will they see the origins of a large and dangerously pathological underclass that has become a tragic and apparently permanent feature of American society?

7

Welfare Reform Must Address the Crisis of Illegitimacy

William J. Bennett

William J. Bennett, a former U.S. secretary of education and director of national drug control policy, is codirector of Empower America, a public policy research organization in Washington, D.C.

The welfare system sustains and subsidizes illegitimacy, a condition that causes poverty and social decay, particularly among black Americans. Illegitimate children are more likely to be poor, drop out of school, and become criminals and drug abusers than children in two-parent families. The welfare system contributes to these problems by providing cash grants to mothers who have children out of wedlock. Meaningful welfare reform must include ending aid to mothers who have illegitimate children and reducing the frequency of illegitimacy among America's poor.

Editor's Note: The following viewpoint was a statement given to the House of Representatives Ways and Means Subcommittee on Human Resources on January 20, 1995.

It is a pleasure to address this committee on a subject of enormous importance. Illegitimacy is the single most destructive social pathology in modern American society. I appreciate the committee's decision to focus attention on this issue, and the willingness of many of you to tackle it head-on.

Mr. Chairman, I believe that any meaningful reform of our current welfare system must address the problem of illegitimacy. My statement will thus focus on the significance of the increase in illegitimacy, the attendant human cost, and the role of our current welfare system in sustaining and perpetuating illegitimacy.

From William J. Bennett's statement to the House Ways and Means Committee, Subcommittee on Human Resources, January 20, 1995.

March 1995 marked the 30-year anniversary of "The Negro Family: The Case for National Action"—also known as the Moynihan Report, one of the most important pieces of social science ever produced.

This 78-page report, authored by Daniel Patrick Moynihan, now the senior senator from New York but then an assistant secretary at the Department of Labor, concluded that "[The break-up of the black family] is the single most important social fact of the United States today. . . . At the heart of the deterioration of the fabric of Negro society is the deterioration of the Negro family. It is the fundamental source of weakness of the Negro community at the time. . . . The family structure of lower class Negroes is highly unstable, and in many urban centers is approaching complete breakdown."

When the Moynihan Report was made public, *Newsweek* magazine referred to its "stunning numbers." The *New York Times* editorialized that "whatever the index of social pathology . . . it is apparent that the Negro family in the urban areas of this country is rapidly decaying." William Ryan of Harvard (one of Moynihan's most prominent critics) warned of "frightening statistics about broken Negro families, illegitimate Negro children, and Negro welfare recipients." Martin Luther King, Jr. categorized the existing breakdown of the Negro family as a "social catastrophe."

That was then. Consider now. In 1991, 68 percent of all black births were out-of-wedlock. Only 6 percent of black children born in 1980 will live with both parents through age 18, according to some projections. And more than 70 percent of black children will have been supported by AFDC [Aid to Families with Dependent Children] payments at one point or another during childhood. In testimony at a Senate Finance Committee hearing chaired by Senator Moynihan, Professor Lee Rainwater predicted that by the end of the twentieth century out-of-wedlock birthrates for minorities will be 80 percent, while the out-of-wedlock birthrate for Americans as a whole will be 40 percent.

Children in single-parent families are six times as likely to be poor as those in intact families, and far more likely to stay poor.

The Moynihan Report had little to say about the white family save that "the white family has achieved a high degree of stability and is maintaining that stability." Alas, that stability has now dissolved. During the intervening 30 years, white family structure has been severely eroded by high rates of illegitimacy, divorce, desertion and welfare dependence. White illegitimacy, for example, has increased from 4 percent in 1965 to 22 percent in 1991. The percentage of white females who are divorced has risen sharply. If these trends continue they will have even more serious consequences for American society than the decline of the black family, since whites constitute a much larger segment of the U.S. population.

This rapid, massive collapse of family structure is without precedent among civilized nations. Our country cannot sustain it; no country can. The American public in general—and the black community in particular—

would surely give its collective eyeteeth to wake up one morning and again face the "frightening statistics" of 1965. Mr. Chairman, the committee should consider this question: what words can adequately describe the situation we are now in? If "social catastrophe" described the situation three decades ago, what words can possibly describe our much worse situation now?

The Moynihan Report places our current social situation in historical context, and it clearly reveals two things: one is that the nation has taken a ruinous social slide over the last three decades. The other is that we have become in many ways inured to the trauma.

The human cost

One thing we need to guard against is viewing these out-of-wedlock birthrates as sterile or abstract numbers. Behind these numbers there are real-life stories and tragedies and wasted lives. Although single women can do a fine job raising children—my mother was divorced and raised my brother Bob and me—it is a lot harder to do it alone. And we know that the chances of successfully raising children in a single-parent home are not nearly as good as raising children in a two-parent home. Every civilized society has understood the importance of keeping families together. They have known, too, that you cannot raise young boys to become responsible citizens unless there are other good men in their lives—men who will spend time with them, discipline them and love them.

There is a large economic dimension to illegitimacy. Children in single-parent families are six times as likely to be poor as those in intact families, and far more likely to stay poor. Consider just two Census Bureau facts: (1) the family income of black two-parent families is almost three times the family income of white single-parent families; and (2) children in white single-parent families are two-and-a-half times more likely to be living in poverty than the children in black two-parent families. The 1991 median family income for two-parent families was $40,137. For divorced mothers, it was $16,156. And for never-married mothers, $8,758.

But there is more—much more—than economics involved. Children in single-parent families are more likely to drop out of school, do poorly while they are in school, have emotional problems, become criminals, use drugs, be a victim of violent crime, and be physically and sexually abused. In short, we are producing a lot of "at risk" kids. And as John J. DiIulio, Jr., professor of politics and public affairs at Princeton University, wrote, "They become juvenile and adult violent crime victims and criminal predators. They end up jobless and on welfare. They do drugs and get sick. A high fraction of the black males finish life in prison (nobody visits) and dead (nobody mourns) well before their time."

One of the reasons that I have some confidence in the direction the nation is heading on welfare is that increasingly there is agreement on two important premises. The first is the widespread acceptance of overwhelming empirical evidence: the current system is a complete failure. We have spent enormous sums—$5 trillion—over the past three decades on welfare programs, and what do we have to show for it? An underclass which is much larger, more violent, more poorly educated and which consists of many more single-parent families.

The second area of agreement is on an important moral principle: having children out-of-wedlock is *wrong*. Not simply economically unwise for the individuals involved, or a financial burden on society—but morally wrong. Even Secretary of Health and Human Services Donna Shalala, she of impeccable liberal credentials, said in an interview that "I don't like to put this in moral terms, but I do believe that having children out-of-wedlock is wrong." I hope that the administration and the Congress enact legislation which is intellectually consistent with that analysis.

The relevant question for this committee, then, is the degree to which welfare programs have (unwittingly) promoted illegitimacy. I think a strong case—a commonsense case—can be made that it has contributed a lot. Welfare may not cause illegitimacy, but it does make it economically viable. It sustains it and subsidizes it. And what you subsidize you get more of. Welfare is illegitimacy's economic life-support system.

The debate is over

I believe that the intellectual debate about the role of welfare in fostering illegitimacy is essentially over. President Bill Clinton helped end it when he said in an interview that "I once polled 100 children in an alternative school in Atlanta—many of whom had had babies out-of-wedlock—and I said, 'If we didn't give any AFDC to people after they had their first child, how many of you think it would reduce the number of out-of-wedlock births?' Over 80 percent of the kids raised their hands. There's no question that [ending welfare for single mothers] would work. The question is . . . is it morally right?" That *is* a good question—to which the answer is "yes." It is morally right because many more people would live better if we scrapped the current system, which subsidizes out-of-wedlock births.

I believe that making adoption easier is an essential and compassionate part of welfare reform. Adoption is the best alternative we have to protect a child's interest in a post-welfare world. The demand is virtually unlimited (at least for very young children), but current laws make adoption exceedingly difficult. Lifting restrictions on interracial adoption and easing age limitations for adoptive parents will help ensure that large numbers of children will be adopted into good, stable, loving homes. And for older children we must invest generously in the kinds of congregate care and group homes that provide order and love.

I will admit that there are no easy answers on this issue; every reform will involve some social dislocation. The fact is, no policy proposal is free of a potential downside. Unfortunately, we have inherited a disaster.

My own view is that ending welfare is prudent and humane—prudent because the social science evidence is in: illegitimacy is the surest road to poverty and social decay. And welfare subsidizes and sustains illegitimacy. It is humane because, again, many more people would live far better lives if we scrapped an entire system that subsidizes out-of-wedlock births. Here's "tough love" on a large scale: end welfare, and young girls considering having a baby out-of-wedlock would face more deterrents, greater social stigma and more economic penalties arrayed against them if they have babies. There would, therefore, be far fewer births to unwed mothers, and far greater life opportunities for those girls.

I applaud the Republican majority [in Congress] for taking serious steps toward dismantling the current welfare system. That you are willing to re-examine the core assumptions of current welfare policy is very good news indeed, as is the fact many Republicans are challenging the idea that AFDC, housing subsidies and food stamps should retain their status as open-ended entitlements. While I don't embrace every part of the welfare proposal outlined in the "Contract for America" [ten reforms proposed by the 1995 Republican-led Congress during its first one hundred days], I believe it is a good start. It is far better than what we have now.

There are a number of sound policy options from which to choose. I would very much like to see a radical devolution of power—that is, return power, money and responsibility back to the states, those "laboratories of democracy," where the most innovative and impressive reforms are taking place. I think that you'll agree that the governors have a far better track record than the Congress when it comes to implementing genuine welfare reform. I have outlined here some of the broad policy outlines which I would like to see states embrace. But we should give states the freedom to experiment; what works in Utah, after all, may not work nearly as well in New York.

The social science evidence is in: illegitimacy is the surest road to poverty and social decay.

We are now engaged in a vigorous debate about the best means to reform welfare. But it is important that we keep in mind the end-game; namely, sometime soon we want welfare to end. When it does we can judge those policies, and their broad social implications, against reality.

Mr. Chairman, our welfare system is the most pernicious government program of the past quarter century. (It is also, ironically, one of the most well-intentioned.) We have lost large parts of an entire generation because of the terrible human wreckage left in its wake. Enough is enough. It's time to pull the plug. For the sake of the children.

Let's get to it.

8

Welfare Should Be Eliminated

Michael Tanner

Michael Tanner is the director of health and welfare studies at the Cato Institute, a libertarian think tank in Washington, D.C.

The welfare system wastes money and is unfair to all Americans, including the five million families receiving Aid to Families with Dependent Children (AFDC). Substantial evidence proves that there is a link between the availability of welfare and out-of-wedlock births, that welfare contributes to increased crime, that job-training programs are ineffective, and that government policies cannot improve the behavior of welfare recipients. The welfare system—including AFDC, food stamps, subsidized housing, and other assistance programs—cannot be reformed and should be eliminated.

From across the political and ideological spectrum, there is almost universal acknowledgment that the American social welfare system has been a failure. Since the start of the War on Poverty in 1965, the U.S. has spent more than $3.5 trillion trying to ease the plight of the poor. The result of that massive investment is, primarily, more poverty.

The welfare system is unfair to everyone: to taxpayers, who must pick up the bill for failed programs; to society, whose mediating institutions of community, church, and family increasingly are pushed aside; and, most of all, to the poor themselves, who are trapped in a system that destroys opportunity for them and hope for their children.

Pres. Bill Clinton deserves credit for bringing this issue back to the forefront of the public policy debate. Yet, both liberals and conservatives seem unable to understand the fundamental structural failure of welfare. Liberals continue to believe that throwing more money at current (or new) programs will make them work, while conservatives search for a paternalistic set of "incentives," such as "workfare" and "LEARNfare." Neither of those approaches is likely to solve the problems of the American social welfare system.

It is time to recognize that welfare cannot be reformed. It should be ended. There may be relatively little that can be done for people already on welfare. The key issue is to avoid bringing more people into the cycle of welfare, illegitimacy, fatherlessness, crime, more illegitimacy, and more welfare. The only way to prevent new people from entering the failed system is to abolish programs that insulate individuals from the consequences of their actions.

The origins of modern welfare

The origins of the modern social welfare system probably can be traced to the Social Security Act of 1935. Best known for establishing Social Security and unemployment insurance, that law, passed during the heart of the Depression, also contained a number of means-tested joint Federal-state programs to provide temporary assistance to certain categories of the poor. They included Old Age Assistance, Aid to the Blind, and—most important—Aid to Dependent Children, the forerunner of Aid to Families with Dependent Children (AFDC).

Those initiatives were intended to have a very limited application. Aid to Dependent Children, for instance, was designed to assist a small number of widows and children whose fathers had died. Even those limited programs represented a significant change in social welfare policy. Previously, social welfare had been considered not a government responsibility—certainly not the Federal government's—but the domain of families, churches, fraternal organizations, and other private charitable entities. The Social Security Act, with its attendant programs, represented the first major step on the road transferring responsibility for helping the poor from the private to the public sector.

However limited their original purpose, government social welfare programs inexorably began to expand. By the mid-1950s, many of those receiving welfare benefits were not widows. Many never had been married. A new class of individuals dependent on government support had been created. Criticism mounted. By the early 1960s, *The New York Times* was editorializing that "the problem [of poverty] cannot be solved with a welfare check."

As a result, a shift began in the emphasis of social welfare programs, from cash payments designed to support people to those designed to lift people out of poverty. An entire new group of training, education, and other noncash programs was born.

It is time to recognize that welfare cannot be reformed. It should be ended.

Social welfare spending exploded, beginning with the Economic Opportunity Act of 1964. Pres. Lyndon Johnson introduced a new generation of public programs, including Medicaid and food stamps. By the end of the 1960s, virtually every low-income American was eligible for some sort of publicly funded assistance.

Also during the 1960s a subtle shift in the public perception of social welfare developed. Public aid began to be seen not as a form of tax-supported charity, but as an "entitlement." That trend culminated with the 1970 U.S. Supreme Court decision in *Kelly v. Goldberg*, which held that welfare benefits were "an entitlement protected by the due process clause" of the Constitution.

There was little change in the growth of welfare until the Reagan Administration began to tighten eligibility requirements in the mid-1980s. Ronald Reagan attempted, on a program-by-program basis, to restrict eligibility to the "truly needy." States were required to set eligibility and income-verification standards. Nevertheless, total welfare spending continued to grow, and benefit levels remained relatively stable.

Promoting jobs instead of welfare

The last major attempt at welfare reform was the Family Support Act of 1988. The centerpiece of that effort was the Job Opportunities and Basic Skills (JOBS) Training Program, a combination job-training and job-search initiative. States were allowed to mandate that individuals participate in job-search and could require some participants to perform community-service work as a prerequisite for receiving benefits. The legislation's chief sponsor, Sen. Daniel Patrick Moynihan (D.-N.Y.), said of the legislation, "For 50 years the welfare system has been a maintenance program. It has now become a jobs program."

Despite the work requirements, the percentage of AFDC recipients participating in job-search, job-training, or community-service work ranges from a high of 30% in Utah to a low of less than one percent in Hawaii. Nationwide participation averages just 6.9%. Predictably, liberals contend that the failure is due to lack of funding, while conservatives claim the work requirements never have been enforced sufficiently.

Today, there are more than 100 overlapping Federal anti-poverty programs, including 59 major means-tested ones. For example, there are 12 different programs providing food, administered by five separate Federal departments and one independent agency. There are seven housing programs, administered by seven separate departments. That does not count state and local bureaucracies.

Approximately 5,000,000 families receive AFDC. Nearly one of every seven American children is in a family receiving such aid. More than 20% of all those born in the late 1960s have spent at least one year on welfare; over 70% of African-Americans born during the same period have done so. Moreover, the situation is growing worse. More than 30% of all children born in 1980 will spend a year on welfare, and in excess of 80% of African-Americans.

Sixty-four percent of welfare recipients are white; 31%, African-American; 14%, Hispanic; and 5% are classified as "other." Ninety-two percent of families on welfare have no father present. The average family size is 2.9 persons, down from four in 1969.

Welfare dependence is increasingly multigenerational. Although the majority of children raised in AFDC households will not receive AFDC themselves, the rate of AFDC dependence for those raised on that program is far higher than for their non-AFDC counterparts.

Perhaps the gravest social challenge facing America today is the skyrocketing increase in out-of-wedlock births, which have increased by more than 400% since 1960, when 5.3% of all births were out of wedlock. Among whites, 2.3% were out of wedlock; among blacks, 23%. By 1990,

28% of all births were out of wedlock. The rate among whites had increased to 21%, and among blacks, to 65.2%.

The rate of out-of-wedlock births to teenagers nearly has doubled in the past two decades. Out-of-wedlock births per 1,000 unmarried women have increased faster for women aged 15 to 19 than for any other age group.

The concern over the increased rate of out-of-wedlock births is not a question of private morality. If TV's Murphy Brown were typical of unwed mothers, objections would be far more muted. However, only 4% of out-of-wedlock births to white mothers are to women with college degrees, while 82% are to females with a high school education or less. Women with incomes of $75,000 or more are responsible for 1% of white out-of-wedlock births; those with family incomes under $20,000, 69%.

Having a child out of wedlock often means a lifetime in poverty. Approximately 30% of all welfare recipients become such because they have an out-of-wedlock child. The trend is even more pronounced among teenage mothers—50% go on welfare within one year of the birth of their first baby and 77% within five years of his or her birth. Nearly 55% of AFDC, Medicaid, and food stamp expenditures are attributable to families begun by a teen birth. This does not include the cost of such other social programs as special education, foster care, and public housing subsidies.

Moreover, once on welfare, those women find it very difficult to get off. While the average length of time spent on welfare is relatively short, generally two years or less, 65% of those enrolled in the program at any given time will be on the program for eight years or longer. Single mothers make up the largest portion of long-term recipients, averaging 9.33 years on welfare and making up 39.3% of all recipients on welfare for 10 years or longer.

The non-economic consequences of out-of-wedlock births are equally stark. There is strong evidence that the absence of a father increases the probability that a youngster will use drugs and engage in criminal activity. According to one study, children raised in single-parent families are one-third more likely to exhibit anti-social behavior than those raised in two-parent families. Another study found that, holding other variables constant, black children from single-parent households are twice as likely to commit crimes as black children from families whose fathers are present. Nearly 70% of juveniles in state reform institutions come from fatherless homes.

Moreover, the situation perpetuates itself. White females raised in single-parent households are 164% more likely to bear children out of wedlock than those who grew up in two-parent households. Children raised in single-parent families are three times more likely to become welfare recipients as adults.

Obviously, any public policy that encourages out-of-wedlock births is a failure. Yet, that is exactly the situation with the current U.S. social welfare system. The evidence of a link between the availability of welfare and out-of-wedlock births is overwhelming. As early as the 1960s, it was recognized that the perverse incentives of welfare were likely to have a negative impact on the family structure of recipients.

More recently, a study for the U.S. Department of Health and Human Services found that an increase in monthly welfare benefits led to an increase in out-of-wedlock births. Holding constant a wide range of variables—including income, education, and urban vs. suburban setting—the study found that a 50% increase in the value of AFDC and food stamp payments led to a 43% growth in the number of out-of-wedlock births. Research by Shelley Lundberg and Robert Plotnick of the University of Washington showed that a rise in welfare benefits of $200 per month per family increased the rate of out-of-wedlock births among teenagers by 150%.

Nearly one of every seven American children is in a family receiving [Aid to Families with Dependent Children].

There are some who dispute any link between welfare and out-of-wedlock births. They point out, for instance, that Louisiana and Mississippi have approximately the same rates of out-of-wedlock births as does California, but have much lower AFDC benefits. That would appear to contradict the argument that high welfare benefits lead to more out-of-wedlock births. However, the actual rate of AFDC payments is of far less importance than the value of the entire welfare package within the context of the local economy. In that context, the welfare packages essentially are equal. Therefore, it is not surprising that they yield similar rates of out-of-wedlock births.

Presumably, women do not get pregnant just to get welfare benefits, and a wide array of other social factors has contributed to the growth in out-of-wedlock births. Nevertheless, by removing the economic consequences of an out-of-wedlock birth, welfare has taken away a major incentive to avoid such pregnancies. A teenager looking around at her friends and neighbors is likely to see several who have given birth out of wedlock. When she sees that they have suffered few visible consequences (the very real consequences of such behavior often are not immediately apparent), she is less inclined to modify her own behavior to prevent pregnancy.

Until young women, particularly those living in relative poverty, can be made to see the real consequences of pregnancy, it will be impossible to gain control over the problem of out-of-wedlock births. By disguising the consequences, welfare makes it easier for those girls to make the decisions that will lead to unwed motherhood.

Current welfare policies seem to be designed with an appalling lack of concern for their impact on out-of-wedlock births. Indeed, Medicaid in 11 states actually provides infertility treatments to single women on welfare.

Once the child is born, welfare also appears to discourage the mother from marrying in the future. Research by Robert Hutchins of Cornell University shows that a 10% rise in AFDC benefits leads to an 8% decrease in the marriage rate of single mothers. Since marriage is the number-one way women escape welfare, it is easy to see that welfare increases the long-term dependence of single mothers.

Economic incentives to remain on welfare

Contrary to stereotypes, there is no evidence that people receiving welfare are lazy. Rather, the choice of welfare over work often is a rational decision based on the economic incentives presented. The combined tax-free value of welfare benefits is roughly equal to the income that can be earned at many entry-level or low-paying jobs. In addition, an individual leaving welfare may have to forfeit medical and child-care benefits. Thus, for many, welfare may seem a perfectly reasonable alternative to work.

Most welfare recipients lack the skills necessary to obtain the types of jobs that pay top wages. As Douglas Besharov of the American Enterprise Institute explains: "The average annual earnings for female high school dropouts are extremely low. In 1992, 18- to 24-year-old dropouts working full time earned about $12,900 a year. . . . Even with the help of the current Earned Income Tax Credit (EITC) and other means-tested programs, earners at these levels net, after payroll and state taxes and work expenses, only $15,563. . . . The major expansion of the EITC pushed through by President Clinton, when fully implemented in 1996, raises these numbers to $17,022. . . . But this increase will not be enough to break the hold of welfare.

"A welfare mother without any work experience probably couldn't match even these earnings. But if she could, she still might decide it didn't pay to work. Her current benefits—even ignoring the $4,307 in Medicaid for which a welfare recipient with two children is eligible—leave her only some $2,674 worse off than the low salaried mother. . . . In other words, should she be lucky enough to get the type of job held by others of her educational attainment, she'd be working for a net wage of only $1.50 per hour."

While it would be nice to increase the wages of entry-level employees to the point where work pays better than welfare, government has no ability to do so. Attempts to mandate wage increases, such as minimum wage legislation, result chiefly in increased unemployment. Therefore, it is likely that the value of welfare will continue to eclipse the value of work. Perhaps that is why 68.6% of welfare recipients report that they are not actively seeking employment.

Welfare and crime

In February 1994, the Maryland State Conference of the National Association for the Advancement of Colored People released a report concluding that "the ready access to a lifetime of welfare and free social service programs is a major contributory factor to the crime problems we face today." Research for the U.S. Department of Health and Human Services showed that a 50% rise in the monthly value of combined AFDC and food stamp benefits led to a 117% increase in the crime rate among young black men.

Welfare contributes to crime in several ways. Children from single-parent families are more likely to become involved in criminal activity than are those from two-parent families. As welfare contributes to the rise in out-of-wedlock births, it concomitantly contributes to the associated criminal activity.

Welfare leads to increased crime by contributing to the marginalization of young black males in society. As George Gilder, author of *Wealth and Poverty*, has noted, "The welfare culture tells the man he is not a necessary part of the family," a process Gilder says is being "cuckolded by the compassionate state." He describes the typical inner city today as "almost a matriarchy. The women receive all the income, dominate the social-worker classes, and most of the schools. But a matriarchy is contrary to nature, so what happens is that gangs of young men rule the society. . . . If men don't dominate as husbands and fathers, then they form violent gangs and dominate as thugs and muggers and drug lords."

The role of marriage and family as a civilizing influence on young men long has been discussed. Whether or not strict causation can be proven, it has been shown that unwed fathers are more likely to use drugs and become involved in criminal behavior than are married fathers.

Moreover, when those pathologies are concentrated within a single community, crime increases still further. For example, research indicates a direct correlation between crime rates and the number of single-parent families in a neighborhood.

Welfare contributes to crime in several ways.

There are those who object to criticism of the welfare system as a "new paternalism," a form of behavioral modification measure aimed at eliminating immorality among poor women. Certainly, there is an odor of paternalism about some conservatives. For instance, Robert Rector of the Heritage Foundation calls for "legislation requir[ing] responsible behavior as a condition of receiving welfare benefits."

Many conservative approaches to welfare reform tend to be punitive in nature or designed to micromanage the behavior of poor people. Michael Schwartz of the Free Congress Foundation Center for Family Policy explains it this way: "Responsible behavior (marriage) should be rewarded, irresponsible behavior (out-of-wedlock childbearing) should not." Some conservatives would extend the system of reward and punishment far beyond questions of marriage and childbearing. For example, Wisconsin Gov. Tommy Thompson's LEARNfare proposals require that the children of welfare recipients attend school as a condition of their parents' receiving benefits, and Rector has called for conditioning welfare benefits on childhood immunization. Nearly all conservative welfare reform proposals link benefits to some form of work requirement.

Conservatives are correct in understanding the way welfare has distorted behavior in ways that generally are damaging to recipients and their offspring, but oddly, many conservatives then turn to government for solutions. They maintain that government can devise a proper mix of incentives and disincentives, rewards and punishments, that can cause poor people to act according to some predesigned plan of behavior.

The larger conservative agenda becomes clear in some welfare proposals that would fund massive government programs to teach abstinence or greatly would restrict the availability of divorce. Thus, welfare reform becomes merely a building block in the conservative call for a "moral and cultural renewal."

Setting aside the philosophical issue of whether it is a proper role of government to attempt to mold citizens' behavior, the government has been remarkably unsuccessful in developing ways to change underclass behavior. One very popular among conservatives is workfare, the requirement that welfare recipients perform public-service jobs in exchange for benefits. The belief is that such jobs will give the recipient both work experience and incentive to get off welfare. However, the types of employment envisioned under most workfare programs are unlikely to give recipients the experience or job skills necessary to find employment in the private sector. For example, New York Mayor Rudolph Giuliani wants welfare recipients to perform such jobs as scrubbing graffiti and picking up trash from city streets. It is difficult to imagine graffiti scrubbers learning the skills needed to put them in demand by private employers. There seems little difference, therefore, between the sort of work program and the type of government-guaranteed jobs program traditionally decried by conservatives. Another problem is that workfare soon runs headlong into the desire expressed by some conservatives that women with young children stay home, rather than enter the workforce.

Martin Anderson, former senior economic adviser to Pres. Ronald Reagan, sums up the simple illogic of workfare: "If people are on welfare then, by definition, those people should be unable to care for themselves. They can't work; or the private sector can't provide jobs enough. That is supposed to be the reason they are on welfare. What sense does it make to require someone to hold a job who is not able to work?

"The idea of making people work for welfare is wrongheaded. If a person is capable of working, he should be ineligible for welfare payments. Instead of requiring men and women who are receiving fraudulent welfare payments to work, we should simply cease all payments."

Workfare's justification

Ultimately, the justification for workfare comes down to an emotional appeal to an innate sense of justice, a feeling that no one should get something for nothing, but public-service jobs are not free. The Congressional Budget Office estimates that each public-service job creates $3,300 in monitoring costs. That does not include potential child-care outlays of up to $3,000 per participant, if mothers with young children are included. That is a great deal of money to spend for psychic satisfaction.

A second welfare reform much ballyhooed by conservatives is LEARN-fare, a requirement that the children of welfare recipients attend school as a condition of their parents' receiving benefits. Thompson, who pioneered LEARNfare in Wisconsin, says he did so to "keep teenagers in school and make welfare recipients more responsible parents."

LEARNfare appears to have little impact. To start with, it may have been unnecessary. Children of parents receiving AFDC are no more likely to miss school than are other kids. Moreover, LEARNfare does not appear to increase the likelihood that youngsters will stay in school. A multi-year evaluation, conducted by the University of Wisconsin, showed no improvement in either attendance or graduation rates of those covered by the program.

Conservatives should recognize that government is not capable of managing behavior. Instead of trying to develop a mystical combination of rewards and punishment, America would be much better off simply removing programs that insulate individuals from the natural consequences of their actions. It reasonably could be expected that people, faced with the consequences of their actions, would change their behavior. Such an approach would avoid coercion and the conceit that government knows best.

There is little evidence that job training actually works.

Meanwhile, a small core of unreconstructed liberals argues that the nation has failed to provide sufficient funding to make existing social welfare programs work properly. They call for an expansion of existing programs and new investments in job training and child care. For example, the Working Off Welfare Act, sponsored by Rep. Lynn Woolsey (D.-Calif.), would triple funding for JOBS and expand child-care assistance, while forbidding states to cut AFDC benefits.

The liberals are correct in noting that AFDC benefits have not kept pace with inflation in recent years, but that is only one component. The total benefits package has remained relatively constant.

There currently are a host of government job-training programs. The Department of Education alone runs 59 different job-training programs at a cost of $13,000,000,000. The Labor Department runs 34 more programs, costing $7,000,000,000. Almost every government agency, from the Agriculture Department to the Appalachian Regional Commission, seems to offer at least one.

There is little evidence that job training actually works. A 1987 study by the General Accounting Office of 61 job-training programs in 38 states concluded that they "are helping recipients find only dead-end jobs, and are failing to give the poor the education and training they need to advance."

It is difficult to determine the success of various job-training programs because most state officials who administer them do not attempt to monitor such things as the proportion of trainees who actually leave welfare, whether they remain off welfare, and whether their income actually increases. What is known is far from encouraging.

Child care

Liberal approaches to welfare reform also call for a heavy investment in child-care services. Sandra Hofferth, one of the nation's leading authorities on day care, questions the need for additional government-provided child care. "Analysis of the number of centers and family day-care homes . . . over the past 15 years does not suggest any evidence of a shortage," she indicated in 1993.

Both Federal and state governments have made major investments in child care in recent years. The 1990 Act for Better Child Care created a vast new Federal child-care bureaucracy at a cost of $22,000,000,000. In addition, AFDC contains an open-ended entitlement to provide child care to recipients, including transitional assistance to mothers who lose AFDC eligibility because they have accepted work. Federal spending on that program totaled more than $479,000,000 in 1993. Yet, welfare rolls have not declined.

The evidence also suggests that mothers prefer informal child-care arrangements to the formal licensed day-care centers advocated by those calling for additional funding. There exists today an extensive system of informal day care. While all states license or regulate day-care centers that care for more than six children, there are nearly 1,000,000 small, unregulated neighborhood or family child-care providers, typically a mother caring for one of her own kids along with one or two of her neighbors'. That figure does not include such traditional sources of child care as aunts and grandmothers.

As a result, even when government-funded child care is available, many otherwise eligible welfare recipients choose not to take advantage of the program, preferring relatives and other informal alternatives. For example, Ohio's Learning, Earning and Parenting (LEAP) Program offered subsidized day care to teen mothers while they attended school or other education programs, but fewer than 20% of eligible mothers reported using LEAP-funded child care.

Rather than establish vast new Federal child-care initiatives, it would be better to reform the current Child Care and Child Development Block Program to allow a greater choice of providers, including neighbors, relatives, and church-run centers. Where localized shortages exist, government should be seeking to remove regulatory barriers that are artificially limiting the availability of providers.

Liberals, together with many conservatives, also have called for toughening enforcement of child-support requirements. While the concept of requiring fathers to support their children has broad support, there is considerable question about whether such action significantly will reduce the welfare rolls. Many, if not most, unwed fathers are poorly educated, lack job skills, and earn little or no regular income, especially when their children are young. Thus, while vigorous child-support enforcement may help women who end up on welfare because of a divorce, it is unlikely to significantly affect the problem of long-term dependence of unwed mothers.

The President deserves enormous credit for advancing the welfare debate. His courage in confronting the special interests in his own party has made possible the discussion of ideas that never have been realistically on the table before. In much the way that only Richard Nixon could have gone to China, only Clinton could have called for a time limit on welfare.

In actually crafting an alternative, though, he has been less successful. Despite good intentions, the President's approach [the Work and Personal Responsibility Act of 1994] appears to borrow the worst ideas of both liberal and conservative reforms. The centerpiece is a two-year time limit for welfare eligibility, during which recipients would receive job training. At the end of the two years, those individuals removed from welfare would be required to obtain work in the private sector or perform public-service jobs.

As already has been seen, the record of government job-training initiatives is not bright. Moreover, the President's plans for job-training assistance may do little good for welfare recipients who are most at risk for long-term dependence—teen mothers. The problem becomes even more acute if, as reported, the program initially will target recipients aged 25 or younger. Eighty percent of teen mothers are high school dropouts. Two years of job-training are unlikely to prepare them to obtain work in a competitive private-sector economy.

A study by the National Commission for Employment Policy of a small-scale pilot program similar to the Clinton plan did provide evidence that such an undertaking could help some welfare recipients move from welfare to work. The study focused on women over the age of 22, though, a group very unlike that targeted by the Clinton plan. Older recipients already are the most likely to leave the welfare rolls within two years, even without government assistance. The problem group of teen mothers was not addressed.

Public-service jobs are no solution

If, after two years, welfare recipients are unable to find jobs in the private sector, publicly funded community-service jobs will be necessary. The Administration estimates that between 500,000 and 1,000,000 public-service jobs could be required. The enormous cost is one reason the President has begun to scale back his proposal.

The ultimate problem with the Clinton plan may be that it focuses primarily on people already receiving welfare, most of whom will move off welfare within two years whether or not government intervenes. There may be relatively little that government can do to move those who already are trapped in long-term dependence off welfare—short of simply kicking them off. Therefore, it seems more important to concentrate on preventing new people from entering the system

The Clinton plan actually may encourage people to enter the welfare system. It establishes new benefits and, since people may be eligible for those benefits only if they are already on welfare, it becomes a rational decision for the low-income working individual, currently making a marginal living, to quit work and enter the welfare system. A study of a job-training program in Oregon, offered under the 1988 Family Support Act, found that welfare rolls grew significantly after the training program became available. Moreover, the study concluded that the new enrollees were "individuals who previously qualified for AFDC but did not apply for benefits and/or people who reduced their employment to qualify for AFDC."

The Republican majority in Congress, meanwhile, has brought its own agenda. Their workfare proposals are unlikely to be any more successful than Democrat ideas.

If both liberal and conservative welfare reforms are unlikely to work, what will? The entire social welfare system for individuals able to work should be eliminated. That includes AFDC, food stamps, subsidized housing, and all the rest. Individuals unable to support themselves through the job market should be forced to fall back on the resources of family, church, community, or private charity.

We should not pretend that such changes in our social welfare system will come easily or painlessly. In particular, ending welfare will be difficult for those who currently use welfare the way it was intended—as a temporary support mechanism during hard times. However, those people—almost by definition—remain on welfare for very short periods of time. Therefore, it should be possible to care for them through other mechanisms.

When it comes to charitable giving, Americans are the most generous people on Earth. Every year, they contribute more than $120,000,000,000 to charity. Surely, the U.S. can find private means to assist individuals who need *temporary* help.

There may be relatively little that can be done for those already on welfare. The key issue is to avoid bringing more people into a cycle of welfare, illegitimacy, fatherlessness, crime, and more illegitimacy. It is the children growing up in the welfare-ravaged neighborhoods who are the true victims of America's social welfare policies.

Adoption must be made a viable option for women who bear children they cannot afford to raise. That will entail eliminating the regulatory and bureaucratic barriers that restrict adoption today. Newt Gingrich's call for putting them in orphanages quickly fostered opposition and laughter, a combination that doomed it to failure.

It also must be ensured that government pursues policies designed to stimulate economic growth and create jobs. That means reducing regulations and cutting taxes to spur progress. Policies that make it more costly to hire new employees should be resisted. Occupational licensing laws and other regulations that disproportionately restrict employment opportunities for the poor also should be eliminated.

We are not going to solve our welfare problems by throwing more money at them.

We are not going to solve our welfare problems by throwing more money at them. Nor will it work to put welfare recipients to work in government-funded jobs picking up trash along the highways. It is time to recognize that welfare cannot be reformed. It should be ended. Some say that would be too cruel, that it would punish the victim—but what could be crueler than sacrificing another generation to our current social welfare muddle?

Organizations to Contact

The editors have compiled the following list of organizations concerned with the issues debated in this book. The descriptions are derived from materials provided by the organizations. All have publications or information available for interested readers. The list was compiled on the date of publication of the present volume; names, addresses, phone and fax numbers, and e-mail addresses may change. Be aware that many organizations take several weeks or longer to respond to inquiries, so allow as much time as possible.

American Enterprise Institute for Public Policy (AEI)
1150 17th St. NW
Washington, DC 20036
(202) 862-5800
fax: (202) 862-7177

AEI sponsors research on a wide range of national and international issues, including economics, government regulation, health care, and taxes. Its bimonthly magazine, the *American Enterprise*, has published articles advocating reform of America's public welfare system.

American Public Welfare Association (APWA)
810 First St. NE, Suite 500
Washington, DC 20002-4267
(202) 682-0100
fax: (202) 289-6555

APWA is an organization of members of public welfare agencies and other individuals interested in welfare issues. The association supports state decisions to implement two-year time limits on welfare benefits and favors sufficiently funded federal block grants to states. Its publications include the quarterly tabloid *APWA News* and the quarterly journal *Public Welfare*.

Bread for the World (BFW)
1100 Wayne Ave., Suite 1000
Silver Spring, MD 20910
(301) 608-2400
fax: (301) 608-2401

BFW is a Christian organization devoted to eliminating hunger and poverty. It maintains the Bread for the World Institute on Hunger and Development, an institute that researches and attempts to influence government policies related to hunger. BFW publishes background papers, the monthly *Bread for the World Newsletter*, and the booklet *Let's Get Real About Welfare*.

Cato Institute
1000 Massachusetts Ave. NW
Washington, DC 20001-5403
(202) 842-0200
fax: (202) 842-3490
e-mail: cato@cato.org

The Cato Institute is a libertarian public policy research organization that advocates limited government. It has published reports calling for an end to the welfare system in its Policy Analysis series and its quarterly *Cato Journal*.

Center on Social Welfare Policy and Law
275 Seventh Ave., Suite 1205
New York, NY 10001-6708
(212) 633-6967
fax: (212) 633-6371

The center is a nonprofit organization that works with and on behalf of poor people to ensure that adequate income support—"public funding provided on the basis of need"—is available to meet the poor's basic needs. It has many publications concerning welfare issues, including the monthly *Welfare Bulletin*, the bimonthly *Welfare News*, and the report "Welfare Myths: Fact or Fiction? Exploring the Truth About Welfare."

Children's Defense Fund (CDF)
25 E St. NW
Washington, DC 20001
(202) 628-8787
fax: (202) 662-3530

CDF promotes the interests of children, especially poor, minority, and disabled children. It supports government welfare programs for poor children and welfare reform proposals that will not deprive these children of assistance. In addition to its monthly newsletter, *CDF Reports*, the fund publishes many books and pamphlets, including the book *The Welfare Reform Debate: Implications for Child Care*.

Coalition on Human Needs (CHN)
1000 Wisconsin Ave. NW
Washington, DC 20007
(202) 342-0726
fax: (202) 342-1132

The coalition is a federal advocacy organization that works in such areas as education, federal budget and tax policy, health care, housing, and public assistance. It lobbies for adequate federal funding for welfare, Medicaid, and other social services. CHN's publications include *How the Poor Would Remedy Poverty* and the bimonthly newsletter *Insight/Action*.

Heritage Foundation
214 Massachusetts Ave. NE
Washington, DC 20002-4999
(202) 546-4400
fax: (202) 546-8328

The Heritage Foundation is a conservative public policy research institute. It is a proponent of limited government and advocates welfare reform that stresses moving the recipient from welfare to private employment. The foundation publishes a variety of articles and papers on welfare reform in its Backgrounder series and in its quarterly magazine *Policy Review*.

National Center for Neighborhood Enterprise
1367 Connecticut Ave. NW
Washington, DC 20036
(202) 331-1103
fax: (202) 296-1541

This organization promotes self-sufficiency in low-income communities and the revitalization of urban neighborhoods. It publishes the periodic newsletter *In the News* and the book *On the Road to Economic Freedom: An Agenda for Black Progress*.

Progressive Policy Institute (PPI)
518 C St. NE
Washington, DC 20002
(202) 547-0001
fax: (202) 544-5014
e-mail: ppiinfo@dlcppi.org

PPI is the think tank of the Democratic Leadership Council, an organization of conservative and moderate Democrats. The institute advocates the elimination of the unconditional entitlement to Aid to Families with Dependent Children benefits and participation in job-training programs, recommending in their place "an employment system that both requires and enables welfare recipients to work." PPI publishes the report "Work First: A Progressive Strategy to Replace Welfare with a Competitive Employment System."

Women's Committee of One Hundred
750 First St. NE
Washington, DC 20002
(202) 336-8345

The Women's Committee of One Hundred represents "a new mobilization of informed women," including activists, elected officials, professionals, and scholars, who are committed to defending women's economic security. The committee publishes the quarterly newsletter *Update* and *Welfare Is a Women's Issue*, a packet of fact sheets on welfare.

Bibliography

Books

Mimi Abramovitz — *Under Attack, Fighting Back: Women and Welfare in the U.S.* New York: Monthly Review Press, 1996.

Helen Blank — *The Welfare Reform Debate: Implications for Child Care.* Washington, DC: Children's Defense Fund, 1996.

Hillary Rodham Clinton — *It Takes a Village and Other Lessons Children Teach Us.* New York: Simon & Schuster, 1995.

Sheila Collins — *Let Them Eat Ketchup! The Politics of Poverty and Inequality.* New York: Monthly Review Press, 1996.

Theresa Funiciello — *Tyranny of Kindness: Dismantling the Welfare System to End Poverty in America.* New York: Atlantic Monthly Press, 1993.

Herbert J. Gans — *The War Against the Poor: The Underclass and Antipoverty Policy.* New York: BasicBooks, 1995.

Sheila B. Kamerman — *Starting Right: How America Neglects Its Youngest Children and What We Can Do About It.* New York: Oxford University Press, 1995.

Gwendolyn Mink — *The Wages of Motherhood: Maternalist Social Policy, Race, and the Political Origins of Women's Inequality in the Welfare State.* Ithaca, NY: Cornell University Press, 1995.

Marvin N. Olasky — *Renewing American Compassion: A Citizen's Guide.* New York: Free Press, 1996.

Virginia E. Schein — *Working from the Margins: Voices of Mothers in Poverty.* Ithaca, NY: ILR Press, 1995.

U.S. Senate Committee on Finance — *Teen Parents and Welfare Reform.* Washington, DC: Government Printing Office, 1995.

Rick Weissbourd — *The Vulnerable Child: What Really Hurts America's Children and What We Can Do About It.* Reading, MA: Addison-Wesley, 1996.

Periodicals

Doug Bandow — "Welfare Reform Doesn't Go Nearly Far Enough," *Conservative Chronicle*, June 12, 1996. Available from PO Box 11297, Des Moines, IA 50340-1297.

Peter Barnes — "Welfare Is Integral to Our System," *Los Angeles Times*, March 13, 1995. Available from Reprints, Times Mirror Square, Los Angeles, CA 90053.

David T. Beito — "Poor Before Welfare," *National Review*, May 6, 1996.

Robert Friedman — "The Welfare Maze," *Life*, January 1996.

George Gilder   "End Welfare Reform as We Know It," *American Spectator*, June 1995.

Jane Haddam   "Promote the General Welfare!" *Nation*, January 29, 1996.

Jesse Jackson   "Shuffling Welfare Cards Isn't Enough," *Los Angeles Times*, May 26, 1996.

Liz McCloskey   "Perspective on Welfare," *Commonweal*, February 23, 1996.

Daniel Patrick   "Congress Builds a Coffin," *New York Review of Books*,
Moynihan   January 11, 1996.

Katha Pollitt   "Devil Women," *New Yorker*, February 26–March 4, 1996.

Progressive   "Real Welfare Bums," March 1996.

Joe Sexton   "Poor Communities Fear Drain If Welfare Is Cut," *New York Times*, February 8, 1996.

Michael Slate   "When My Baby's Hungry—Makes Me Want to Hurt a Lot of People," *Revolutionary Worker*, April 14, 1996. Available from PO Box 3486, Merchandise Mart, Chicago, IL 60654.

Jodeen Wink   "Listen: True News of a Welfare Mother," *Humanist*, September/October 1995.

Ann Withorn   "The Politics of Welfare Reform: Knowing the Stakes, Finding the Strategies," *Resist*, April 1996. Available from One Summer St., Somerville, MA 02143.

Stephen T. Ziliak   "The End of Welfare and the Contradiction of Compassion," *Independent Review*, vol. 1, no. 1, Spring 1996. Available from 134 98th Ave., Oakland, CA 94603-1004.

Index